IN ALL THINGS
13 weeks of devotions from Africa

Written by
Christian authors of Africa

SHIRLEY CORDER
ASHLEY WINTER
ANNA JENSEN
YVONNE TIPPINS
CRYSTAL WARREN
DERYN VAN DER LANG
DIANNE J. WILSON
VAL WALDECK
VIDA LI SIK
ANN GOODFELLOW
MARION UECKERMANN

Copyright
All Rights Reserved.

13 Books as Follows:
7 African Animals © 2020 Shirley Corder
What God Wants © 2020 Ashley Winter
Musings from an African Garden © 2020 Anna Jensen
Life is Good © 2020 Yvonne Tippins
Steps of Faith © 2020 Crystal Warren
Sunrise to Sunset © 2020 Deryn van der Tang
Seven Lights for Dark Times © 2020 Dianne J. Wilson
Seven Saints in Lockdown © 2020 Val Waldeck
Promises to Cherish © 2020 Vida Li Sik
Inspired to Worship © 2020 Ann Goodfellow
Poems from an African Garden © 2020 Anna Jensen
Seven Reflections from the Ocean © 2020 Marion Ueckermann
Peace in Life's Storms © 2020 Shirley Corder

Amazon Paperback: Independently Published March 2021

ISBN: 9798722744876

Imprint: Independently published

eBook Edition: October 2020 Limited Edition

South Africa paperback © December 2020 Limited Edition: Copies may be purchased direct from the authors.

ISBN: 978-0-620-91231-0

Visit Shirley at her website, shirley@shirleycorder.com

Contact information: shirley@shirleycorder.com

Please note that this paperback book was initially created as a boxed set of e-books. These have now been compiled into the one book you hold in your hands. Each section of the compilation starts with the cover (in black and white) of the individual seven-day book.

Acknowledgements

In addition to the acknowledgements stated in the relevant sections, I'd like to express grateful thanks to all the authors who have come together to make this set possible. Your enthusiasm, encouragement, and positive vibes have made this challenge a joy.

Thank you to all those who proof-read each individual book after it was "final." It's amazing how many little things you picked up. Without your willing help, this collection would not have reached the standard I believe it has. So thank you especially to Vida Li Sik, Val Waldeck, Crystal Warren, and Allyson Koekhoven.

Thank you to those who have offered to read through the entire set of books when it was finished, ever searching for those gremlins that creep in when the authors and editors are not looking!

A special vote of thanks to Anna Jensen and Marion Ueckermann. You have stood alongside me, brainstorming ideas and adding your creativity and expertise throughout the project.

Mostly, all thanks and praise to the author and creator of all our lives, and of the wonderful land of Africa, our Heavenly Father who is always there...*In All Things*.

To God be all the glory!

In All Things
13 Weeks of Devotions from Africa

Introduction

The continent of Africa is a land of majesty, mystery, and magnitude like no other. Truly, it is a world within one continent. And God is *In All Things*—hence the title of this compilation of devotional books.

When this idea came into being, it was shared with the writers of CWOSA (Christian Writers of Southern Africa) and I asked for interested volunteers. The response was immediate and heartwarming.

Why thirteen sets of devotions? And why seven days per author? Because that comprises three months of reflections, with each week offering seven devotions on a theme, different, but all linked to Africa.

The authors were all born, raised, or are now living in Africa, so we have strong ties to this wonderful but turbulent land.

Authors were asked to come forward with a theme they felt the Lord wanted them to write on, and that in itself was an amazing event. There were no repeat suggestions. Wild animals to beautiful gardens, amazing sea-scapes to rugged landscapes, poetry to personal experience—and many more.

Because we are a potpourri of authors, some born or brought up in other lands, some born and raised in Africa before moving to far-off lands, and some who have lived their entire lives in South Africa, you will find our Englishes vary! Some have written in British English, others in

American English, and some in South African English which is close to British. For that reason, each book will mention which English is being used—limiting the choice to British or American. So please don't let an apparent incorrect punctuation mark or spelling detract you from the message.

We would encourage you to read a devotion a day, which will last you three months. However, if you just can't resist reading straight through, do go back and read them daily in order to get the most out of each meditation.

It is our prayer that you will be blessed by our insights and drawn closer to the wonderful God who is *In All Things.*

7 *African Animals*
and what they teach
us about God

Shirley
Corder

7 AFRICAN ANIMALS

© 2020 Shirley Corder
All Rights Reserved.

Cover Art © Shirley Corder
Cover Image Kudu © Jamie Muller @ Unsplash
Praying Hands: coolvectorstock @ 123rf
Africa Icon: Shirley Corder

Edited by Paula Bothwell @ PBProofreads

These devotions are written in American English. Where African terms are used they are clarified.

Newsletter

Would you like to be among the first to know when a new book is coming out?

Sign up for my newsletter and you will receive:

◦A free book

◦Snippets of personal news

◦Updates on my latest writing project

◦Sneak Peeks into my books

◦Recommended reading material

◦Occasional free offers or competitions

Emails normally only come to you every two weeks or longer. I will not fill your inbox with SPAM, nor will I pass on your address to anyone else. You may also unsubscribe at any time. Sign up on my website.

Visit me at my website, https://shirleycorder.com
Or contact me at writetoinspire@shirleycorder.com:

Acknowledgments

Grateful thanks as always to **my husband, Rob,** for all his encouragement and for freeing up so much time for me to write.

Huge thanks to **Dianne Marie Andre** for her critiques, edits, and friendship, from across the world.

Thank you to those who beta-read or edited this book: **Shirley Crowder, Judith Robl, Arlene Johnson, Dianne Marie Andre, Rob Corder.**

Thank you to **Paula Bothwell** @ PBProofreads for doing the final edit.

Thank you to all **the photographers** who make the result of their talents available to the public on the Internet.

Thank you to **the members of my Book Brigade** who encourage me and help me to get the word out about my books.

Mostly, all thanks and praise to my **Heavenly Father** who created me with a plan, and is always there to guide and direct me to become the person He wanted me to be.

To all those who care for our magnificent African wildlife. Thank you for your loyalty and concern for these creatures that have little or no protection against the brutality of illegal hunters and poachers.

"The Lord God made them all."

Table of Contents

Introduction

Africa is the second-largest continent in the world and is home to many unique and majestic animals. Whether we look at the ginormous elephant with its gentle family relationships, the massive buffalo with its mafia tendencies, or the hideous hyena that seems to find life a joke, we can only marvel at the complexities of creation—and the wonder of the God who created them all.

The purpose of this small book is to give you material for seven days of devotional readings. In the process, you will learn about seven amazing creatures of Africa, five of whom are collectively known as the Big Five, not only because of their size, but because they are known to be highly dangerous, and, sadly, it is considered a feat for trophy hunters to bring parts of them home. You will see God's hand at work in the way they live, survive, and interact with nature; and you'll receive encouragement to draw close to the God who not only created these animals, He created you.

Take your time over each chapter. Ponder any questions. And allow each animal to draw you closer to your Creator God.

The Big Five share excerpts from my book, *God in Africa ~ 90 Days in the Land of Majesty & Mystery.* Enjoy your visit to Africa!

-1-
Trunk Message

"I pray that he will help you live at peace with each other, as you follow Christ. Then all of you together will praise God, the Father of our Lord Jesus Christ."
(Romans 15:5-6 CEV)

An hour's drive from our home takes us into the Addo Elephant Park. This wildlife reserve houses over ninety species of mammals and is home to over six hundred gentle but gigantic African elephants, the largest of the Big Five.

One exceptionally hot, sunny afternoon, we were parked with dozens of other vehicles, watching a vast herd of elephants gathered around a large, muddy waterhole. It was a delight to observe several groups of young elephants romping together in the water or in the muddy slush at the water's edge.

Suddenly, a drama was enacted in front of us as two young bulls challenged each other in a show of dominance. After much trumpeting and clashing of tusks, the loser of the two turned and plodded away from the herd, his ears flapping in anger—right into the paths of the parked cars.

All the drivers managed to reverse their cars out of its path but we were caught between two reversing vehicles, and ended up sitting frozen as this angry bull thumped his massive form straight toward us. I desperately wanted to lift my camera and take a photo, but I was terrified of attracting his attention. He was already irate. I didn't want to do anything to annoy him further. We sat motionless as he stomped past our car, so close I could have stroked him through the window if it had been open. I had my camera on my lap, lens upward, and gently pressed the button with no idea where it was pointed. Down the one side of our vehicle he plodded, then appeared to think twice of his decision. As we watched in the side mirrors, we saw him turn behind our car and return on the driver's side on his way back to the herd.

As he moved away, we decided we'd had enough elephants for the afternoon, and moved onto the road that would take us to the exit. When I got home, I was thrilled to discover I had the most incredible photograph on my camera. All it showed was a part of his head and one eye with amazingly long eyelashes. And that eye was looking straight into the camera!

Elephants are highly intelligent animals with excellent memories. The belief that they never forget is not correct. However, they do have strong abilities to recall people, places, and behavior. Another fallacy is that they are scared of mice. They do, however, have very poor eyesight so it is likely that when a mouse darts past, the big beast is startled.

These most sociable of animals live in large family groups. Researchers can identify greeting ceremonies, defense rituals, vocal communication, social play, parenting skills, and threat displays.

Because of their size and their close family bonds, elephants have only two real threats. The first is selfish, greedy human beings who kill them for their massive, much-coveted, ivory tusks. The second is drought, which can cause the death of these enormous creatures that eat about three hundred pounds of vegetation in a day and drink a bathtub full of water. In their weakened state, they become extra vulnerable to other predators.

There is usually one leader, the matriarch, who is often the oldest female in the family. The rest of the herd may be made up of her own offspring. She teaches them how to protect themselves from danger, and she guides them to safe places to find food and water. The males leave the herd during their adolescent (teen) years and often form small groups of their own, although they usually keep an eye on the family.

Their strange, long noses, called trunks, are super-sensitive to all types of movement or sensation. They use them for smelling, breathing, drinking, grabbing tree branches, and trumpeting. They communicate with one another over long distances and can call for help for miles using signals on sound waves that can often only be heard by fellow elephants.

Community for the elephant is extremely important. This serves as a reminder that no matter how big or powerful we may be, we still need one another. Who makes up your community? Is it only your family? In today's society, chances are your family is wide-spread. My family ranges from Montenegro in Europe, to Idaho in the United States of America, to a number of provinces in South Africa. Much though I love them, can I really call them my community? My neighbors, fellow church members, our currently locked-down senior choir—that is my community.

How about you? Can you think of ways you can improve your relationships with those around you, and draw them into your community? Those living close by are in the same situation as you. They need that bond of fellowship as much as you do.

 Lord, help me to be sensitive to the needs of those around me and do all I can to build up the community of believers.
In Jesus' Name,
Amen.

-2-

Remember the Kudu

"Praise be to the Lord, the God of Israel, because he has come to his people and redeemed them. He has raised up a horn of salvation for us."
(Luke 1:68-69)

I caught my breath as two extremely long spiral horns showed above the dense wilderness of the African *bushveld*. My husband slowed the car to a crawl as we edged forward, both of us watching intently, looking for the owner of these magnificent trophies. Seconds later, we saw him.

The enormous antelope, the kudu, stood tall and majestic, head held high, lazily chewing his cud while watching us with cautious eyes. His instinctive wariness was justified, as his species is approaching extinction. Greedy hunters kill for his horns, which may be anything up to seventy-two inches (1,82 meters) in length if stretched out.

"His horns have two-and-a-half twists," I whispered, knowing this meant he was a fully mature male. The horns start to grow once the bull is approaching one year old, with their first full twist at around two years.

We sat in awe, knowing how blessed we were to have such an amazing up-close sighting, as these beautiful creatures are notoriously hard to approach. They are highly alert animals, quick to detect danger with their large, radar-like ears. I have never heard the sound, but I believe they call out with a hoarse alarm bark at the sign of danger, before fleeing to safety.

The horn has been found to make an outstanding bugle, and its beautiful sound can be heard over a great distance. The kudu's horn is frequently used to make the shofar which is blown as part of the Jewish Rosh Hashanah and at the end of Yom Kippur. So those same horns that can lead to the animal's untimely demise can be used in beautiful worship of their Creator.

Take a look at your hands. They too can be used to bring about disaster in your life, yet they can be raised in praise to the One who created the kudu, the animals of Africa . . . and you.

The kudu is one of the largest and most beautiful of all antelopes. There are two species of kudu: the "greater kudu," such as the one we were admiring, and the "lesser kudu," a smaller relative only found in East Africa. We sat motionless in the car, scared to move in case we frightened this stunning creature away. I quietly snapped one shot with my camera, careful not to move more than necessary.

Their Zulu name is onomatopoeic: *Umgakla.* It imitates the sound of the clashing of horns when two of these great animals fight ferociously during mating season. They charge each other like olden-day knights—a sight I believe is both awesome and terrifying to watch.

Sometimes, during a fight, their immense spiral horns lock together and they are unable to disengage. When this happens, they cannot feed or get to water, nor can they protect themselves against prowling predators. Ultimately, they will both die.

Is it not sad to imagine these magnificent beasts dying in such a tragic way, starved to death or destroyed by predators that they could easily have outrun, if they hadn't got trapped through their fight with another kudu? Can you think of a situation in your own life, or do you know of one, that can compare to this? One where those involved are trapped in a situation of their own making, unable to break loose?

From this tragedy, the Zulus in the past developed a saying, *"Remember the kudu!"* They use the expression even today as an illustration of the futility of war, where there are no true winners. Both sides lose so much. When their hot-headed young people want to dash into conflict without giving thought to the consequences, their elderly parents or grandparents may well say to them, "Remember the kudu, my child. Remember the kudu."

Are there times in your life when you're inclined to rush in and get into an argument or worse, enter into an argument, possibly because of your pride, where you really have no hope of winning? How can you avoid the heartache that can result? Maybe you also need to *"remember the kudu!"*

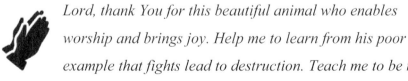 *Lord, thank You for this beautiful animal who enables worship and brings joy. Help me to learn from his poor example that fights lead to destruction. Teach me to be more patient and loving. In Jesus' Name, Amen.*

-3-
The Animal Mafia

"Will the wild buffalo condescend to serve you, volunteer to spend the night in your barn? Can you imagine hitching your plow to a buffalo and getting him to till your fields?"
(Job 39:9-10 MSG)

The Cape African buffalo is one of the Big Five amazing animals of Africa, along with the lion, rhino, leopard, and elephant. They are also the most powerful animal. These non-territorial beasts live in mixed herds of up to one thousand. They can occasionally be seen throughout southern, central, and eastern Africa.

Lethal in their own right, buffalos are second only to hippos in the hierarchy of dangerous African animals. When they feel threatened, buffaloes attack their prey with their massive horns, giving no prior warning of their impending ambush. Having few natural predators, if they do come under an obvious threat, the mighty animals band together in a tight gang. They show no fear and, when faced with their mob mentality, even lions flee.

We were thrilled to one day spot a huge army of them lined up in front of dense bush in a reserve. We knew to keep our distance, but I saw for myself what I had previously only read about. As we viewed them through binoculars, the males seemed to stare straight at us with an expression of intense dislike. Truly unnerving. Could they really see us? And why did they hate us so much?

Way back in history, after the buffalos had charged and killed more humans than any other animal, they were given the nickname *Black Death*. They usually circle and stalk their prey until the right moment to strike, then they tear apart their opponents with their massive, thick horns.

The buffalo are often referred to as the *animal mafia*. Where elephants are purported to never forget, the buffalo never forgives. They often seek revenge on someone who threatened them years before. The animals also hang out together in very large and intimidating mobs. An adult may weigh around 1,540 pounds (700 kg) and even lions will not normally attempt to take down a buffalo.

In the book of Job, God Himself speaks about the buffalo. He stresses that although this animal is a mighty beast, you can never rely on a buffalo! *"He's hugely strong, yes, but could you trust him, would you dare turn the job over to him? You wouldn't for a minute depend on him, would you, to do what you said when you said it?"* (Job 39:11-12 MSG).

Surprisingly, considering the size of a buffalo, they are strong swimmers who will cross deep rivers for better grazing. The herds are subdivided into clans of about a dozen cows and their offspring, all under one leader. This guide buffalo is responsible to lead his group to water and food even during times of drought. He walks in front with the rest of

24

his herd following closely behind. If it weren't for the leader's knowledge and guidance, the beasts would perish.

If a herd of buffalo comes under threat, they form a circle around their young. All the adults face outward and lower their heads, forming a protective and intimidating barrier with their fearsome horns. Similarly, in ancient Roman warfare, as in Jesus' day, soldiers frequently used the *testudo*, or a tortoise formation, during battles. The soldiers formed a tight pack, with the back rows holding their shields over the heads of the ranks. Together, they formed an impenetrable wall of protection, much like the buffalo's defense system.

For an enemy to take on a well-formed Roman army against this wall of shields was a death sentence. Together in formation, the soldiers were a highly disciplined and dangerous opposition. But if the aggressors managed to break their formation, the soldiers became vulnerable. Whereas their armor covered most of the front of their bodies, their backs were exposed. So they depended on one another for protection against the enemy. If an attacking army was able to break the formation, they could win the battle.

This is also true of the African buffalo. No one in their right mind, not even a lion, would attack a herd (or obstinacy) of buffalo in formation. But if one is separated from the pack, the herd becomes vulnerable, and then a couple of lions may attack.

The African buffalo and the Roman soldiers share the principle of operating in protective formation against an enemy. Do you see similarities between their approach and the way the Christian army of believers today should operate? Unfortunately, the Christian army has been described as the only one that attacks fellow soldiers from the back. Have you seen evidence of this?

As Christians, where is our strength when facing opposition from the devil? The buffalo or the soldier who is out of his formation is vulnerable. As a Christian, how vulnerable are you? Especially at times of isolation, such as during the COVID pandemic, or for missionaries in foreign lands, what steps can Christians take to maintain their positions in the Body of Christ?

Lord, help me to stay in formation with other Christians. This is particularly difficult during times such as the battle against COVID-19 where many churches are not physically able to meet together. Help me to keep in contact with my community, and also to protect those who are isolated.

In Jesus' Name,

Amen.

4

Tough yet Sensitive

[God said to Noah,] "You are to bring into the ark two of all living creatures, male and female, to keep them alive with you."
(Genesis 6:19)

Africa is the proud home of the rhinoceros, usually known as the rhino. After spending several days in a game reserve in Africa, my husband and I had seen all the "Big Five" except the elusive rhino, the second largest land mammal on earth. Then, on our last day, we saw two in the distance. I was thrilled to capture them with the zoom lens of my camera.

There are two varieties of rhinos: the white rhino and the critically endangered black rhino. Surprisingly, their names have nothing to do with color. In fact, they came about as a result of a linguistic mistake! The Dutch immigrants to Southern Africa soon noticed that one type of rhino had wide, flat lips which they used to graze on the dry ground, tearing up the sparse, coarse grass. The other kind had a hooked upper lip which they used to pick fruit from branches and select leaves from twigs. So the settlers differentiated between them by calling the former the *Weid Mond Rhino*, meaning wide-mouthed rhino.

Along came the English settlers, and they misunderstood and thought the Dutch were calling them *white* rhino. And so the two got their names: the white rhino and the black rhino—despite being the same dark gray in color. There are, in fact, quite a few differences between the two sets of cousins. The white rhino is considerably larger than the black and has a distinctive barrel-shaped body. The black rhino is smaller and has a more compact build.

Both types of rhino are widely and illegally poached for their horns. These are believed to have medicinal properties and have a similar value to gold on the black market. Vietnam, where the horns are ground for drinking, is the biggest buyer. Hunters frequently slaughter these beasts only for their horns which are, in fact, nothing but keratin, the same protein found in our fingernails.

There is nothing more tragic than the occasional video released of a baby rhino crying next to its butchered and bled-to-death mother. The calves are severely traumatized by these events, and it takes skilled nurturing from trained carers to nurse them through to adulthood.

Until recently, the white rhino was on the edge of extinction. However, it has made a remarkable comeback as a result of persistent conservation efforts, and is now classified as "near extinction." The black rhino, however, is one of the world's animals closest to extinction. You rarely see either kinds of rhinos outside of national parks and reserves.

For all their differences, one thing both the cousins share, however, is their temperament. These cantankerous beasts are extremely mistrustful of strangers and will not let anything stand in their way. Very little can withstand a charging rhino. Even railway locomotives have been derailed when rhinos saw them as threats.

We probably all know of someone who is like a rhino, quick to lose his temper, and flying into a rage if threatened. On a scale of 1 (placid) to 10 (easily provoked), how would you rate your temper?

Scientists have come to realize that during stressful times, such as the current period of lock-down, our minds work overtime. What used to be a simple trip to the store involves so many decisions. "Have I got my mask? My sanitizer? Do I need a visor? Is that shopping center safe . . .?" During all the time in the store, our minds endure a constant, "Don't touch! Keep a safe distance! Why is that woman wearing her mask under her nose? How can I avoid her?" And finally, when we get home, there is the need to sanitize everything. "How do I sanitize fresh lettuce? Should I soak these or spray them? Is soapy water sufficient or do I need to spray the apples? Isn't that poisonous?" On and on and on . . . we are plagued with constant decisions, never-ending pricks of irritation. I think all of us at times threaten to become like rhinos!

Rhinos love to wallow in the mud. The mud helps them cool down but also dries on their skin, helping to protect them from bothersome insects. Surprisingly, despite their thick skin, they frequently suffer from bug bites and from sunburn.

Despite their heavy build and bombastic nature, rhinos have one particularly weak spot. Their feet are extremely sensitive. In the wild, they typically put most of their weight on their toenails to protect the pads. However, in zoos their toenails often wear down on the concrete surfaces which make them susceptible to infection.

It's hard to picture the tough-skinned, bad-tempered rhino as having sensitive feet, isn't it? How do bug bites, sunburn and sensitive feet make you feel? Is it possible that these three factors contribute toward the rhino's temper? Relating back to the "rhino" in your life, perhaps he or she has an area of sensitivity that really irritates them and there is a reason for their moodiness. Try and identify those areas. See if you can understand their temper triggers, and ask yourself if there is something you can do to help.

Perhaps even more important, the example of the rhino can serve as a personal checkpoint. What areas of sensitivity in your life cause you to become unreasonable or irritable? How can you best deal with those areas? Is there an area of over-sensitivity that you should perhaps pray about?

 Father God, forgive me for the times I am moody or lose my temper, perhaps for no apparent reason. Help me to reach out to others with the same problem.

In Jesus' Name,

Amen.

No Laughing Matter

"The LORD has done it this very day; let us rejoice today and be glad."
(Psalms 118: 24)

One evening, my husband, three young children, and I were holidaying in a cottage on the slopes of a *kopje*, a small rocky hill in the African veld. It was during the violent and bloody guerrilla war raging in Rhodesia, so we were on high alert. In the early evening, we sat outside enjoying some family time after our evening *braai*. Suddenly, an unearthly cackle broke through the gentle background hum of night sounds.

"Wh-what's that?" one of my sons gasped, moving closer to his dad.

"It sounds like a hyena. But it's far away." He'd no sooner spoken than the one voice was joined by an eerie cacophony of howls and laughter.

"What are they laughing at?" my daughter asked, her voice trembling.

When the laughter was challenged by a mighty roar in the night, we unilaterally picked up our plates and drinks and headed inside, leaving my husband to make sure the fire was completely out. Even when settled inside with the door securely locked and the windows shuttered, I kept hearing the echo of that uncanny wicked cackle—whether the sound was real or just imprinted in my mind.

I knew that the hyena's laugh is really no laughing matter. It is a sign of stress—of fear, or aggression. Or they are having a feeding frenzy. Because the scavengers never know when they will eat next, they gorge themselves when the chance presents itself—laughing all the time.

The fact that we'd also heard a lion roar indicated the possible source of their stress. The hyena is one of the most dangerous of a lion's predators. A lone hyena will never normally attack a lion, but a pack of them will—especially if it's an isolated lion or a mother with cubs. Hyenas know if they attack as a pack, they can circle the mighty beast and wear it out with their constant darting around and snapping at the big cat's flesh, all the time howling and laughing in apparent glee, although their laughter doesn't necessarily mean that they're happy. It's just something built into their makeup. Can this perhaps be a challenge to us as Christians?

In Disney's famous movie, *The Lion King*, a trio of hyenas takes the part of the secondary antagonists in the attempt to kill off Mufasa, the reigning king, and Simba, the heir to the animal throne. It is easy to see why Disney chose hyenas for the part. They look scrappy and vicious with their wide staring eyes and their big mouths open in a maniacal grin, drooling with saliva.

Hyenas have a bad reputation as poachers and scavengers, and yet they are perfectly capable of catching their own prey. These dog-like carnivores are found mainly in the southern part of Africa but can be seen elsewhere on the continent as well. While they resemble wild dogs, they are not canines.

There is an interesting side to the personality of the hyena. The keeper of a pair in the Perth Zoo tells how the hyenas have learned to understand the medical procedures they go through on a regular basis. They will stand patiently on scales as well as allow the keepers to apply ear cream and even administer vaccinations. She also tells how these savage animals can actually be surprisingly affectionate toward the people who care for them regularly.

The female hyenas stay with their young longer than any other carnivore, and they will do battle against any other animal that may threaten their young. Mothers will face nearly certain death at the fangs of hungry lions to protect her babies. And even when under attack, they deliriously laugh all the time, in what *appears* to be a state of happiness.

Who are you looking to today, to bring you happiness? Are you trusting in politicians? Or medical experts? Are you relying on a vaccination to COVID-19 to bring sanity to the future? Or are you able to face the future with an unexplainable joy?

Our world is constantly changing. Often our plans get thrown without any notice. How can we allow God's Spirit to fill us with joy even when faced with disappointment or anger or fear? Crises, tragedy, and invisible viruses can bring chaos and uncertainty to our lives. But if we place our hope in the Lord, we can find hope, peace, and even joy—despite our difficult circumstances.

Oh Lord God, when I am stressed, the last thing I want to do is laugh. Please help me to put my trust firmly in You and claim the joy that only You can give.
I ask it in Jesus' Name,
Amen.

-6-

Different Spots

"Come now, let us settle the matter," says the LORD. "Though your sins are like scarlet, they shall be as white as snow; though they are red as crimson, they shall be like wool."

(Isaiah 1:18)

We almost missed it. Our car was parallel with a broad tree branch holding the magnificent beast when I spotted a slight movement out of the corner of my eye. A large leopard lazed on the branch, one leg hanging down as his tail swished casually back and forth.

I knew that despite being rarely seen, thanks to their elusive nature and their excellent camouflage, this member of the Big Five family is actually the African big cat with the biggest distribution.

When I got home, I did some research to find out the difference between the markings of a cheetah, a jaguar, and a leopard. They all have spots. However, I learned that the leopards' spots are actually rosette-shaped on their bodies while they have solid black spots on their heads, legs and sides. Although the common leopard is a tawny color, there are also black leopards. These still have spots, but they aren't visible.

These large beasts are extremely fast and can reach speeds of thirty-six miles per hour (58 kph). They can also leap forward nearly twenty feet, or six meters, the length of three adult humans lying head to feet! These solitary animals each own a territory easily identified with scratches on trees and urine scent marks. Their amazing agility and strength helps them climb trees while dragging a fresh kill, which they do to prevent scavengers, such as the hyena, from stealing their meal. The carcass may be heavier than the leopard's own body weight.

A nocturnal animal, the leopard does its hunting at night. It stalks its prey carefully and when it is close, it pounces and takes down its victim with a bite to the throat.

Like our domestic cats, leopards growl when angry and purr when happy and relaxed. Studies have revealed that they are generally afraid of humans and therefore avoid them. If you ever encounter a leopard when out walking, you are advised to avoid its gaze at all costs. It relies on its camouflage and will remain motionless in the hope that you will not see it. You need to back away slowly, but never break into a run. If you look it in the eye, it knows you've seen it. It has to react—the so-called "flight or fight" response. I hope I never have to put that theory to the test!

As members of the human race, we are all born with various spots of sin that tend to recur. We may become frustrated in our efforts to gain a victory over them—especially in the case of an addiction. "I just can't stop!" people will cry when they want to change their habits. And yes, it's true that we cannot change recurring sins with our own strength. But through the power of the Holy Spirit, strength and guidance of Jesus, and the loving correction of our Heavenly Father, we can.

We may not be able to change our spots. But God can. I once had an ugly spot on my carpet in a prominent place which I couldn't remove. Then one day, I spotted a bottle of liquid in a grocery shop advertised as "Carpet Spot Remover." I bought some and couldn't wait to give it a try. On returning home, I read the label and followed instructions. Wonder of wonders! The spot was gone.

If you have an ugly spot in your life, you may not be able to remove it. But there's One who can. One Spot Remover! And His Name is Jesus.

Scripture tells us: *Can you ever change and do what's right? . . . Can a leopard remove its spots? If so, then maybe you can change and learn to do right* (Jeremiah 13:23 CEV).

In our own strength we cannot change our skin color, nor can the leopard change his spots. But there is hope if we have spots that need to be removed from our lifestyles. Can you identify one spot you wish to get rid of? One issue that spoils your appearance as a child of God?

Take it to The Spot Remover, and ask Him to deal with it, and to show you how to prevent it returning.

 Father God, in the same way a leopard cannot change its spots, nor can I. Thank You that You can change them for me. Please help me to allow You to bring change into my life where it is needed.

In Jesus' Name,

Amen.

-7-

King of the Jungle

"Then one of the elders said to me [John], 'Do not weep! See, the Lion of the tribe of Judah, the Root of David, has triumphed.'"

(Revelation 5:5)

No book on African animals would be complete without a look at the mighty king of the savannah, the lion—perhaps the best known of the Big Five. Although often erroneously called the King of the Jungle, these animals do not, in fact, live in the jungle at all, but in Africa's grasslands and plains.

The male lion, with his majestic mane, is the head of the family and is protective of his pride or following. His regal appearance and royal swagger have earned him the nickname, *King of the Beasts*. His intimidating roar can be heard for many miles.

On several occasions, I have watched these big cats from my vehicle inside a wild game reserve as they lazed on the ground after a meal. They look tame and approachable, as if you could step up and pet them. When their cute, cheeky cubs jump all over their dad, they resemble a litter of cuddly kittens. Yet one roar from that mighty throat, and even his kids leap for safety. Tame and approachable, they are not.

Tourists often forget the big cats are predators, and every year I read of some terrible tragedy that occurred when someone climbed from their car to take photographs of a seemingly benign lion sunning himself. Too quickly the great beast has leaped up and destroyed the misguided photographer.

In Scripture, Peter likens the devil, Satan, to a roaring lion, and there are some clear comparisons. There is a danger when people inside a game park feel safe. They're not. The animals there are just as ferocious as they would be out in the wild. Satan can also appear docile and harmless. He too can sneak up when you're not concentrating and aware of his attempts to lull you into complacency.

If we compare Satan to a roaring lion, we will remember the importance of remaining on the alert, and never letting down our guard. We see that a lion is not to be played with, nor treated lightly. They are wily and sneak up on their prey. In what places might the devil sneak up in disguise in today's world? What about occult practices that are often shown as harmless games or fun things to read in the newspaper? A few years ago, my husband and I were in a lion park with our two teenage grandchildren. We stopped for a few minutes to watch a group of lionesses resting next to the road. A white lioness from the pack wandered calmly around our car and went behind our vehicle. Suddenly, the car bounced.

My granddaughter exclaimed in a whisper, "Oh, my goodness!"

I swung round to meet the piercing blue eyes of a large lioness peering into our hatchback car, with only the rear window between her and my two grandchildren. She had mounted the vehicle with her front paws, then hunched down to see what was inside. My husband immediately pressed his foot on the accelerator to ease the car cautiously forward. But she held us back for a very long minute with her awesome strength before my husband was able to ease the car from her grip. (This led to a number of interesting reactions when we showed the tooth-holes to our insurers the next day!)

How good to remember that, unlike the real lion, Satan is toothless! His roar may be loud and distracting, but no matter what crisis we may face, Jesus, the Lion of the tribe of Judah, will triumph.

If you are driving through Africa, you do not need to fear the lion as long as you remain in your vehicle and behave intelligently. What does this say to us as Christians in our response to Satan? What "vehicle" do we need to remain in? You may receive tooth holes and experience tragedies, but how good it is to know that Satan's destruction is already guaranteed by the death of Jesus on the cross over two millennia ago.

 Lord, forgive me for the times I allow Satan to draw close to me. Thank You for the victory I have over him through You. In Jesus' Name,
Amen.

Do You Know God?

If you look at the amazing animals of Africa, you can only marvel at the Creator who assembled these creatures. They are all so different, yet each species has its own needs and idiosyncrasies. We humans were brought into being by the same Creator. We also have our own needs and characteristics. But not one of us was an accident. Your human parents may not have intended for you to exist, but God did. What's more, He has a special, unique plan for you. All you need do is make sure of your relationship with your Heavenly Father.

One day, you will meet Him face to face. Are you certain you will be accepted into His Kingdom? If you're not one hundred percent sure, please don't put it off one more moment. There is no such thing as an eighty percent elephant! He either is or he isn't the biggest animal on earth. So for you, it is all or nothing. You are a Christian, or you aren't. I encourage you to use the format of A, B, C, D and make sure you get one hundred percent on your salvation score!

Accept that you are a sinner. Scripture tells us we are *all* sinners. Romans 3:23 tells us *"all have sinned and fall short of the glory of God."*

Believe Jesus Christ is the Savior who loved you so much that He gave His life for you. Jesus said, *"I am the way and the truth and the life. No one comes to the Father except through me"* (John 14:6).

Confess to Him that you have not been fully surrendered to Him and ask for His forgiveness. *"If we confess our sins, he is faithful and just and will forgive us our sins and purify us from all unrighteousness"* (1 John 1:9).

Dedicate yourself to the Father as your God, Christ as your Savior, and the Holy Spirit as the Wind beneath your spiritual wings. Jesus said, *"Whoever hears my word and believes him who sent me has eternal life and will not be judged but has crossed over from death to life"* (John 5:24).

You can use your own words, or you can use these:

Father God,

I have done things which have separated me from You. Please forgive me.

Lord Jesus, I believe You are the only way to God.

I give myself to You now, and I ask You to help me follow You for the rest of my life.

Holy Spirit, please lift and support me as I seek to walk closer to God.

From this moment on, I will seek to walk with You and bring glory to Your name.

I ask this in Jesus' name and through the power of the Holy Spirit. Amen.

If you've prayed this prayer for the first time, I would love you to make contact with me. You can email me at writetoinspire@shirleycorder.com or contact me through my website, https://shirleycorder.com.

If you have enjoyed this book, I'd really appreciate you leaving a short review on any site which sells or promotes the book. Thank you!

Keep in touch and hear when I have other books coming out. All you need do is sign up for my newsletter by going here: https://shirleycorder.com/signup

About the Author

Shirley Corder is a retired nursing sister (RN), pastor's wife, and cancer survivor (1997). She is an internationally well-known devotional writer.

She is the author of a number of books, both traditionally and indie published. Many of the books are available in print as well as electronic format. She has also contributed to thirteen anthologies and other books not to mention many devotional and inspirational articles through the years.

Do visit her on her website or drop her an email. She'd love to hear from you.

Shirley and her husband, Rob, enjoy life in the beautiful seaside city of Port Elizabeth, South Africa. They have three married children and are grandparents to six special young people across a wide range of 21 years.

Website: https://www.shirleycorder.com

Amazon: https://amazon.com/author/shirleycorder

Email: writetoinspire@shirleycorder.com

Other Books by Shirley Corder:

N.B. The links attached to each title will take you direct to the page where you can read more, or order the books.

More in the 7-Day Series

God in the Unexpected: In these seven devotional readings, Shirley Corder encourages you to look for God in the Unexpected.

A Mother's Heart: Being a mother isn't for sissies. But in these seven short stories, Shirley Corder shares some life-lessons drawn from her own life that will draw you closer to God, and to your children.

The Boat that Saved the World: God tells Noah He is going to put an end to the human race. It gets worse. He wants Noah to build a boat to start over. How crazy is that? Read the story from Noah's perspective.

Peace in Life's Storms: Scripture tells of many storms that changed the lives of thousands. In this small book, Shirley Corder offers reassurance and guidelines for finding peace as we face a multitude of storms today, including the dreadful COVID-19 pandemic. Also available as part of this boxed set.

God in Africa - 90 Days in the Land of Majesty and Mystery: Available as an Ebook or paperback or the paperback direct from the author. If you want to know the real Africa beyond the extreme images, violence, and hunger narratives often portrayed in the media, then this book is for you.

Strength Renewed - Meditations for Your Journey through Breast Cancer: An encouraging 90-day devotional for those facing cancer. The book is published by Revell Publishers and is available in e-format or paperback.

Out of the Shadow Series

The *Out of the Shadow* stories are creative non-fiction and include inspirational reflections.

EVE ~ Mother of All: Join Shirley as she draws Eve out of the shadow of the garden and shows her as a real flesh-and-blood woman. If you've ever felt overwhelmed by your situation, or faced impossible challenges, this book is for you.

MIRIAM part 1 ~ Devoted Sister: The little girl who watched her three-month-old brother sail in a basket boat on the crocodile-infested River Nile lived her life under the shadow of her younger brother, Moses. If you have a gifted sibling or friend, or if you battle with feelings of inferiority, you will enjoy this book.

MIRIAM part 2 ~ Gifted Leader: As Miriam comes out of the shadow of her two brothers, Shirley shows us how she becomes a gifted leader in her own right. If you have struggled with criticism over a woman's role in the Church, this book is for you.

NAOMI ~ Beloved Mother-in-law: Join Shirley as she eases Naomi out from the shadow of her daughter-in-law, Ruth. If you've faced tragedy or felt afraid for the future, this is the book for you.

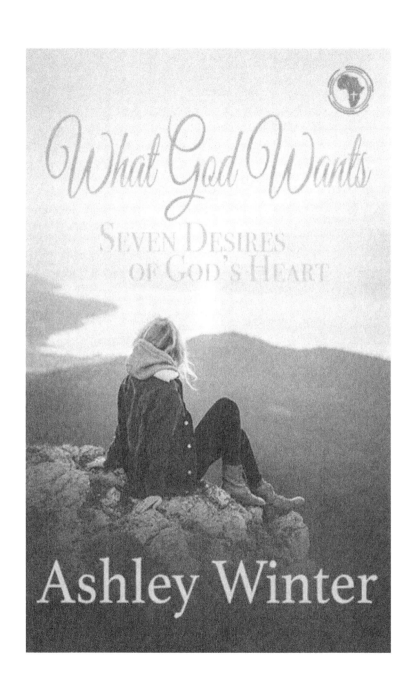

What God Wants

SEVEN DESIRES OF GOD'S HEART

Ashley Winter

WHAT GOD WANTS

Acknowledgements

Photographer: Yaroslav Shuraev
Cover Design: Ashley Winter
Contact Information: ashleywinterauthor@gmail.com
www.ashleyrwinter.com
Find Ashley on Facebook: https://www.facebook.com/ashley.winter
and www.facebook.com/loveinsouthafrica

Table of Contents

Introduction

When I write fictional characters, the question I continually ask myself is, "What do they want?" Their deepest desires speak not only of the essence of who they are, but also of their behaviour. All their actions are driven by these desires. So, in knowing God's desires, we learn the "why" behind His every action, we learn about His nature.

What does God want? Do you know? Have you ever wondered? It's an important question for anyone who seeks to follow Him; a question we should all explore and know the answer to.

The desires of people change. Month by month, day by day, even hour by hour, what we want changes as our circumstances change and our priorities shift. This isn't the case with God. He wanted yesterday what He wants today, what He wants tomorrow and the next day. Our God exists beyond the realm of time. He is our rock eternal, an unchanging constant in a sea of unknowns.

It is a mind-blowing truth – He lets us discover Him, more than that – He *reveals* Himself to us. If we are willing to seek Him with all our hearts, minds and strength, God says that we *will* find Him (Jeremiah 29:13). How astonishing is that?

And if we can truly *know* Him, then we can know His desires. Only in knowing God's desires, can we align *our* hearts and desires with His. The ultimate goal of exploring God's desires, is to make them our own. As we know Him more, what God wants should become what we want. This is what it means to be a follower of Christ. So, let's dive in…

Please note that as a South African, I've written the following devotions in British English.

Desire 1
To be believed in

Isn't it incredible that our God has set up this universe and orchestrated the most awesome redemptive thread throughout history in order to reveal Himself and His great love for us? Our magnificent God *wants* to be believed in. He wants humanity to know beyond all doubt that He exists – that He is real, as real as the intricate creation all around us. He wants us to choose to see Him in everything He has made and done. He wants us to recognise His hand behind every brushstroke of His masterpiece. Simply put, our God wants us to choose to believe in Him. This is faith. This is the starting point, and the foundation for all God's other desires.

"And without faith it is impossible to please him, for whoever would draw near to God must <u>believe that he exists</u> and that he rewards those who seek him" Hebrews 11:6 (ESV).

"For what can be known about God is plain to them, because <u>God has shown it to them</u>. For his invisible attributes, namely, his eternal power and divine nature, have been clearly perceived, ever since the creation of

the world, in the things that have been made. So they are without
excuse" Romans 1:19-20 (ESV).

It is through this spark of faith, the assurance of God's existence, that
a relationship with Him can begin. As simple as it sounds, faith in
something unseen is often far harder for adults to find. Years of a
particular mindset, of acquiring knowledge and theories, along with
experiences of pain and suffering can become a dividing wall which is
difficult to overcome. Even the best scientific arguments as to God's
existence are shrugged off due to this hardening of heart. Apologists
suggest asking the question in this case, "If I could prove the existence of
God to you beyond all doubt, would you believe?"

For many their answer would remain 'no', revealing that their reason
for not choosing faith in God has nothing to do with logical argument. It
is not a 'head' matter, it is a 'heart' matter. They do not *want* to believe.
Yet our Father longs for us to come to Him with the untainted faith of a
child. To drop our years of baggage and run with all our might into His
arms, believing He is real, believing we can know Him personally.

"Now faith is the assurance of things hoped for, the conviction of things
not seen" Hebrews 11:1 (ESV).

"Truly, I say to you, whoever does not receive the kingdom of God like a
child shall not enter it" Mark 10:15 (ESV).

Father, this world throws so many lies at us. Open our eyes to the truth of You. Soften our stubborn hearts to see Your hand behind the wonder of creation. Let us come like open-hearted children into Your arms, knowing You'd never turn us away.

Desire 2
To be known

Although faith is our starting point, God does not want our faith to be without substance – He wants us to truly *know* the One we believe in! This remarkable fact about our God screams that He is not some cold, aloof and distant deity. Our God is deeply personal. Not only does He want us to believe He exists, He also wants us to believe that He *can* and *wants* to be known by us!

"You will seek me and find me, when you seek me with all your heart"
Jeremiah 29:13 (ESV).

From the breathtaking silhouettes of the acacia trees of Africa to the majestic cliffs of the Drakensberg mountains, to the wonder of the Milky Way splayed across the vast heavens, our God reveals the fullness of His nature, His character, His genius, His power and ultimately, His love. He longs for us to seek Him like a thirsty impala seeks out water in a dry place. He longs for us to know Him deeply!

Yet the pinnacle of God's love and desire for us to know Him is not found in creation. His ultimate display of His loving heart is the sending of His Son. Jesus came into the world to reveal His Father to us. All of creation points to God, but Jesus is His exact representation. This is how we can truly know God. Jesus said that if we've seen *Him*, we've seen God, the Father. *(John 14:9)*

"He is the radiance of the glory of God and <u>the exact imprint of his nature</u>, and he upholds the universe by the word of his power" Hebrews 1:3-4 (ESV).

Knowing God is the most precious reward and worthy of our fiercest efforts. This lifelong pursuit begins with accepting His Son as the only way to Father God.

"Jesus said to him, 'I am the way, and the truth, and the life. No one comes to the Father except through me'" John 14:6 (ESV).

Paul, the apostle who wrote half of the New Testament, understood the great value of knowing Jesus. He considered everything in his life worthless in comparison with this treasure.

"Indeed, I count everything as loss because of the surpassing worth of knowing Christ Jesus my Lord. For his sake I have suffered the loss of all things and count them as rubbish, in order that I may gain Christ" Philippians 3:8 (ESV).

"And this is eternal life, <u>that they know you, the only true God, and Jesus Christ</u> whom you have sent" John 17:3 (ESV).

"And we know that the <u>Son of God has come and has given us</u> *<u>understanding, so that we may know him who is true;</u> and we are in him* *who is true, in his Son Jesus Christ. He is the true God and eternal life"* *1 John 5:20 (ESV).*

The Bible leaves no doubt where this is concerned. God the Father wants us to put the faith we have in Him, in Jesus. He longs that we would all come to the knowledge of Him and His great love through His son, Jesus Christ. Faith in Jesus is the way to eternal life.

Oh, that we would truly know You, Father. Give us the discipline to fiercely seek You, to recognise You at work, to dive deeply into Your Word and discover the treasure of who You are.

Day 3
To be loved

Of all the things our all-powerful God could request of us, this one makes it to the top of the Old Testament commandments, and Jesus Himself reinforces it in the New Testament. He wants our love! The God of the universe who whispers and planets are formed, wants you and I to love Him! He is love!

"He answered, 'Love the Lord your God with all your heart and with all your soul and with all your strength and with all your mind'" Luke 10:27 (NIV).

"But if anyone loves God, he is known by God" 1 Corinthians 8:3 (NIV).

The Bible is full to the brim with verses testifying to God's unfailing love for His people. And so, we love Him back because He loved us first!

"We love because he first loved us" 1 John 4:19 (NIV).

"How precious is your steadfast love, O God! The children of mankind take refuge in the shadow of your wings" Psalm 36:7 (ESV).

So how do we love this awe-inspiring God who calls Himself love? Jesus gives us the answer as recorded in Luke's gospel – with all our heart, soul, strength and mind. This is a thorough and complete love, encompassing all of who we are. We love Him passionately, with our emotions, with our thoughts, with all our energy and actions and with the innermost part of who we are. Our God is not looking for empty acts of service, but for every part of us to engage in loving Him. So practically what does this mean for us?

Gary Chapman wrote an insightful book called *"The Five Love Languages"* and you may have heard about it or read it. He suggests there are differences in the ways we each feel loved. Some feel loved when they are given a gift, others need physical touch, still others need words of affirmation, acts of service or quality time. So, what is God's love language, you may ask?

"If you love me, you will keep my commandments" John 14:15 (ESV).

"Jesus answered him, 'If anyone loves me, he will keep my word, and my Father will love him, and we will come to him and make our home with him' John 14:23 (ESV).

God's love language is *obedience*. Now you may think this is a strange way for us to show love to God, but this request from Jesus reveals His heart for us. Like a loving parent and a young child, the parent only wants good things for the child. He instructs him and teaches him the best way, yet the child can choose to ignore the parent's instruction, convinced he knows better. This may end with negative consequences for the child, which would in turn hurt the father. Whatever hurts the child, hurts the father.

And so, our heavenly Father asks us to obey Him and walk in His commands so that we can live free of the consequences our disobedience would bring. In loving Him through obedience we know that He works everything together for our good. What a promise!

"And we know that for those who love God all things work together for good, for those who are called according to his purpose" Romans 8:28 (ESV).

This obedience to God's commands proves our love. Because of our great love for Him, we choose to turn from our own way of doing things, to obey Him and do what pleases Him, with everything we have and all we are.

"I have been crucified with Christ. It is no longer I who live, but Christ who lives in me. And the life I now live in the flesh I live by faith in the Son of God, who loved me and gave himself for me" Galatians 2:20 (ESV).

Father, thank You for Your unconditional love! May we always be in awe of Your presence in our lives. Help us to live surrendered before You daily, in careful obedience to Your every word.

Desire 4

To be worshipped

There is something deep in the heart of mankind that compels us to worship. You may have heard it said that we all worship something, even atheists worship. Some choose ideologies, music, fame, nature, or money as their god. Still others worship their causes, their children or even themselves. God calls this worship of created things idolatry, and it is detrimental to us, not only in this life, but also in the life to come.

So why does God want us to worship Him alone?

And Jesus answered him, "It is written, 'You shall worship the Lord your God, and him only shall you serve'" Luke 4:8 (ESV).

Because He is worthy. God is the only being to exist that was never created. He has always been. He has no beginning and no end. If this were not so, then He wouldn't be God. He exists beyond the realm of space, time and matter.

I love the story of Jesus entering Jerusalem on a donkey. The people welcomed Him with their worship. The Pharisees told Jesus to rebuke them; weren't they breaking the commandment to worship only God? But Jesus refused. He knew what the Pharisees didn't – that being God

Himself, He was worthy of their adoration. In worshipping Him, they were fulfilling the commandment.

"As he was drawing near—already on the way down the Mount of Olives—the whole multitude of his disciples began to rejoice and praise God with a loud voice for all the mighty works that they had seen, saying, 'Blessed is the King who comes in the name of the Lord! Peace in heaven and glory in the highest!' And some of the Pharisees in the crowd said to him, 'Teacher, rebuke your disciples.' He answered, 'I tell you, if these were silent, the very stones would cry out'" Luke 19:37-40 (ESV).

Secondly, *because it benefits us!* Our God knows it is only when *He* takes the prime position in our lives, that we are in safe hands. No other created being or thing could ever love us and lead us like He could.

"My flesh and my heart may fail, but God is the strength of my heart and my portion forever" Psalm 73:26 (ESV).

So how do we worship? Our worship of God isn't an allocated time during a church meeting. It isn't primarily a song or a poem or even a prayer, although these things could be part of it. Our worship of God is in making Him Lord over us. It is the continual laying down of our lives in surrender to Him and His will.

"Therefore, I urge you, brothers and sisters, in view of God's mercy, to offer your bodies as a living sacrifice, holy and pleasing to God—this is your true and proper worship" Romans 12:1 (ESV).

God wants us to worship Him because it is *good for us*, because there is everything to gain! As we lay ourselves down before Him in surrender, knowing that He is good and worthy, and that He loves us, our Father starts to see His perfect Son reflected in us as we are transformed into His image with ever increasing glory. As we worship Him in spirit and in truth, our spirit connects with His and we cry Abba Father (Daddy!). Not only are we affirmed as His sons and daughters in His presence, but we are being transformed into His likeness. This is the life-altering fellowship with the Almighty God and what on earth can compare?

"God is spirit, and his worshipers must worship in the Spirit and in truth" John 4:24 (ESV).

"The Spirit himself testifies with our spirit that we are God's children" Romans 8:16 (ESV).

Father, thank You! Oh, the privilege of being adopted into Your family! May we worship You with everything we are and have, and may You be formed in us so that we reflect Your nature to everyone we meet.

Desire 5
To make us whole

When we surrender our lives to God in exchange for the life we have in Jesus, we as sinful beings don't bring much to the table. Even our finest efforts are like filthy rags. Yet our God chooses to covenant Himself with us in the most unequal arrangement imaginable. He does everything. He gives everything. He fulfils not only His part of the deal, but ours as well, knowing that we aren't able to. And even when we are faithless, He remains faithful, because faithful is who He is—it is part of His nature, and our God doesn't change. How secure are we in our Father's great covenant of love!

We, who were once dead in our sin, are made alive through Christ's sacrifice on the cross. We are transferred from the kingdom of darkness into the kingdom of light – a new creation! We shift from being slaves to being sons and daughters, and heirs with Jesus as we are adopted into God's family. And it is God's desire that *all* people are saved and grafted into this family.

"If we are faithless, he remains faithful— for he cannot deny himself" 2 Timothy 2:13 (ESV).

"All of us have become like one who is unclean, and all our righteous acts are like filthy rags" Isaiah 64:6 (NIV).

"The Lord is not slow in keeping his promise, as some understand slowness. Instead he is patient with you, not wanting anyone to perish, but everyone to come to repentance" 2 Peter 3:9 (NIV).

"Therefore, if anyone is in Christ, the new creation has come: The old has gone, the new is here!" 2 Corinthians 5:17 (NIV).

Yet because of this great love, God doesn't just leave it there. He won't leave us in the state we were when we came to Him, in His mercy He changes us from the inside out. He works powerfully within us to bring about His will and purpose for us. He longs for us to reflect the fullness of His nature, not only desiring to bring wellness to every part of our lives, but also holiness.

"And we all, with unveiled face, beholding the glory of the Lord, are being transformed into the same image from one degree of glory to another" 2 Corinthians 3:18a (ESV).

Our God is holy, and He desires a holy people. 'Holy' simply means 'to be set apart'. He desires that we are blameless at the return of Jesus, and He is faithful to accomplish this in us. The Bible likens the return of Christ to that of a groom coming for his bride – a bride holy and without fault.

"May God Himself, the God of peace, sanctify you through and through. May your whole spirit, soul and body be kept blameless at the coming of

our Lord Jesus Christ. The one who calls you is faithful, and he will do it" 1 Thessalonians 5:23-34 (NIV).

"...and to present her to himself as a radiant church, without stain or wrinkle or any other blemish, but holy and blameless" Ephesians 5:27 (NIV).

What an incredible God we serve! Not only does He reveal Himself to us through His creation, but He makes a way for us to truly know Him, and not only that, He brings us into a relationship with Himself through Jesus, washing away the disobedience that once separated us. And as if this mind-blowing gift wasn't enough, He then covenants Himself to us, transforming us daily into His radiant image. He accepts us as His own children, giving us His name, His beloved church, His body on earth. Then He presents us to Himself as perfect - the fullness of Him, who fills everything in every way.

"And God placed all things under his feet and appointed him to be head over everything for the church, which is his body, the fullness of him who fills everything in every way" Ephesians 1:22-23 (NIV).

Father, words fail us when we think of Your unfailing love for us. We are so undeserving, yet You stoop down to lift us up. You cleanse us. You pay the penalty for our wrong. You heal us and make us whole. You give us Your name, a hope and a future. What love is this? What great, great love!

66

Desire 6
To make us one

As a diverse and once divided nation, South Africans, longing for unity, brought out various slogans over the years in an attempt to bring about much-needed change. One is *'Simunye'* meaning *'we are one'*. Another is *'Ubuntu'* which is roughly *'I am because we are'* and another you may be familiar with is *'The Rainbow Nation'*. It is no secret - there is great blessing in unity. King David wrote about it in the Psalms:

"How good and pleasant it is when God's people live together in unity! [2] *It is like precious oil poured on the head, running down on the beard, running down on Aaron's beard, down on the collar of his robe.* [3] *It is as if the dew of Hermon were falling on Mount Zion. For there the Lord bestows his blessing, even life forevermore"* Psalms 133:1-3 (NIV).

When Jesus prayed for His disciples, He added this precious line:

"Holy Father, protect them by the power of your name, the name you gave me, so that they may be one as we are one" John 17:11 (NIV).

Jesus wasn't praying for everyone when He said this, this prayer was specifically for His church and all those who'd become a part of His church in the future. That we would be united. The challenge of unity is often found in diversity, but so is strength.

The Bible describes this diverse group of believers as many things, but one is a body. Each part has a different function, and we are to respect the contribution that each part brings. Jesus provides us with the key to this in John's gospel.

"By this everyone will know that you are my disciples, if you love one another" John 13:35 (NIV).

I love this. Jesus could have said the world would know we are His disciples because of the miracles we perform or the abundant blessings in our lives, or how righteous we are, but no. It's our love for each other – our love for fellow Christians.

It's caring for aged and frail amongst us and visiting them in hospital. It's providing meals to families who are going through a tough time. It's notes and texts, babysitting, lifts, phone calls and encouragement. It's remembering birthdays, anniversaries. It's rejoicing with those who rejoice and mourning with those who mourn.

As a mother of four, I'm often asked by new moms how I got my babies to sleep through the night early and how I coped as a young mom. So I explain that I was part of a mother's group in our church in Pietermaritzburg, South Africa. The experienced moms would support the new moms so thoroughly, that every baby in the group slept through the night early. All new moms received cooked meals delivered to her house each evening for at least two weeks. As they shake their heads at me in wonder, I tell them that this is how it is in the church. *This* is the church of Jesus!

We are the family of God and it is beyond a privilege to belong to it. It supersedes every race, culture, economic group and nationality. Our brothers and sisters span the globe, our closeness to these otherwise strangers found in the remarkable shared experience of the grace of God in our lives. We are united in common faith, our knowledge of God through Jesus, and His commandment that we love each other deeply.

"Since God so loved us, we also ought to love one another. No one has ever seen God; but if we love one another, God lives in us and his love is made complete in us" 1 John 4:11 (NIV).

"Whoever claims to love God yet hates a brother or sister is a liar. For whoever does not love their brother and sister, whom they have seen, cannot love God, whom they have not seen. [21] *And he has given us this command: Anyone who loves God must also love their brother and sister" 1 John 4:20-21 (NIV).*

Jesus takes this love for fellow believers a step further when He commands that we love our neighbour as we love ourselves. And so this unfathomable love we have for fellow believers is to be shared *outside* the church also! Unbelievers should see it and feel it in and through our lives. This is the boundless love of Christ shared abroad in our hearts.

I was recently challenged by a scripture that I overheard from my husband's morning devotional. God often speaks to us in the strangest ways, but when He does, His truth settles deep.

"Don't just pretend to love others. Really love them" Romans 12:9 *(NLT).*

It's so much easier to go through the motions of what it looks like to love, yet keep the emotion separate from our hearts. And yet we are called to love deeply, in a way that affects us, from the heart.

"Now that you have purified yourselves by obeying the truth so that you have sincere love for each other, love one another deeply, from the heart" 1 Peter 1:22 (NIV).

"And above all these put on love, which binds everything together in perfect harmony" Colossians 3:14 (ESV).

"Above all, love each other deeply, because love covers over a multitude of sins" 1 Peter 4:8 (NIV).

Father, may our hearts be so full of Your love that it spills out to whoever we meet. May others see the life-changing love of Jesus inside us and be changed themselves. Use us as vessels to carry Your transformational love into a desperate world.

7

Desire Us

"Long ago the Lord said to Israel: 'I have loved you, my people, with an everlasting love. With unfailing love I have drawn you to myself'"
Jeremiah 31:3 (NLT).

Everything that God has done since the fall of man has been with this goal in mind – to be with us again. The book of Genesis describes the remarkable scene where God walks through the garden looking for Adam and Eve in the cool of the day. Can you imagine what that must've been like? But for Adam and Eve, this was normal.

When their sin resulted in them having to leave the garden, and live lives separate from Him, our faithful God began His masterful redemptive plan to restore the relationship that was so precious to Him - to conquer the sin that separated us from Him, and the resulting death that sin leads to.

Our God is just, and disobedience cannot go unpunished, yet filled with sin ourselves, man was unable to pay the penalty and live. Animal sacrifices could not pay the penalty, and neither could keeping God's Law. God's Law was merely put in place to lead us to Christ – to show us our desperate need of Him.

"For the wages of sin is death, but the gift of God is eternal life in Christ Jesus our Lord" Romans 6:23 (NIV).

"So the law was our guardian until Christ came that we might be justified by faith" Galatians 3:24 (NIV).

And so the God of the universe came Himself in Jesus and took the punishment meant for us when He died on the cross, so that we can become the righteousness of God through simply believing in Jesus. We take His righteousness; He takes our unrighteousness. This is the great exchange! This is how vast the Father's love for us is!

"<u>See what great love the Father has lavished on us, that we should be called children of God!</u> And that is what we are!" 1 John 3:1 (NIV).

"God made him who had no sin to be sin for us, so that in him we might become the righteousness of God" 2 Corinthians 5:21 (NIV).

When Jesus died on the cross, He died once and for all. He destroyed sin and death, meaning that we are made holy through His sacrifice and we have complete and direct access to Father God. Now there is nothing that can ever separate us from His love!

"For I am convinced that neither death nor life, neither angels nor demons, neither the present nor the future, nor any powers, [39]neither height nor depth, nor anything else in all creation, will be able to

separate us from the love of God that is in Christ Jesus our Lord" Romans 8:38-39 (NIV).

Not only that (as if that wasn't enough!), but death takes on a new meaning. Death is not the end for the believer, we are destined to live and reign with Jesus for all eternity!

"Where, O death, is your victory? Where, O death, is your sting?" 1 Corinthians 15:55 (NIV).

When Jesus ascended to God's right hand in heaven, the Father sent the Holy Spirit to teach, guide and comfort us while on earth, but God's ultimate desire is for us to behold His face and His glory and be with Him where He is. The prayer Jesus prayed before He died reveals the desires of His heart:

"Father, I want those you have given me to be with me where I am, and to see my glory, the glory you have given me because you loved me before the creation of the world" John 17:24 (NIV).

"And if I go and prepare a place for you, I will come again and will take you to myself, that where I am you may be also" John 14:3 (ESV).

Father, how we long to be with You! To gaze upon Your beauty and to see Your glory in all its fullness.

Thank You that we carry your Holy Spirit in us as a deposit, guaranteeing what is to come! And while we wait for the glorious fulfilment of all things, help us to live lives worthy of Your high calling and Your great name.

Psalm 84

[1] How lovely is your dwelling place,
Lord Almighty!
[2] My soul yearns, even faints,
for the courts of the Lord;
my heart and my flesh cry out
for the living God.
[3] Even the sparrow has found a home,
and the swallow a nest for herself,
where she may have her young—
a place near your altar,
Lord Almighty, my King and my God.
[4] Blessed are those who dwell in your house;
they are ever praising you.
[5] Blessed are those whose strength is in you,
whose hearts are set on pilgrimage.
[6] As they pass through the Valley of Baka,
they make it a place of springs;
the autumn rains also cover it with pools.
[7] They go from strength to strength,
till each appears before God in Zion.
[8] Hear my prayer, Lord God Almighty;
listen to me, God of Jacob.
[9] Look on our shield, O God;
look with favour on your anointed one.

¹⁰ Better is one day in your courts
than a thousand elsewhere;
I would rather be a doorkeeper in the house of my God
than dwell in the tents of the wicked.

¹¹ For the Lord God is a sun and shield;
the Lord bestows favour and honour;
no good thing does he withhold
from those whose walk is blameless.
¹² Lord Almighty,
blessed is the one who trusts in you.
(NIV)

About the Author

Ashley Winter is a church-planting wife, mom of four sons (three teenagers!), novelist and award-winning baby photographer. She and her family, though South African, make their home where they feel called by God to be – Swansea, on the beautiful south coast of Wales, UK.

If you'd like to find out more, you can find me at:

Website - www.ashleyrwinter.com

Email – www.ashleywinterauthor@gmail.com

Find Ashley on Social Media.

Novels by Ashley Winter

If you enjoyed this devotional, you might like to take a look at my fiction books. All books within a series follow on and are not stand-alone novels. Click on the series title to go to the Amazon sales page.

"Love in South Africa" Series

Rachel's Blessing
Deborah's Choice
Tanya's Hope
Gemma's Joy
Katherine's Fear
Suzanne's Chance
Isobel's Mercy
Jennifer's Dream
Elmarie's Home
Mariaan's List
Janice's Secret
Lindie's Land
Carolyn's Freedom

Praise for "Love in South Africa"

★★★★★ **Unpredictable and gripping – Shirley Corder**
I bought books 2 & 3 of this series when they were on special, to try out Ashley's books as she was a new writer for me. After reading the first few chapters of Book 2, Deborah's Choice, I rushed to Amazon and bought Book 1, Rachel's Blessing, so I could read from the beginning. I loved the whole story line, the tension at times, the uncertainty at others. I live in South Africa and could visualise each scene of this book. I had great difficulty putting the book down. This is not a traditional boy-meets-girl romance, and the relationship between Rachel and Eric is far from a traditional approach to Christian fiction. But it is true to life. Both the two main characters, as well as the supporting cast, show realistic tussles with their faith-walks. The reader can identify with their struggles, while seeing God's hand at work all the way. Thank you, Ashley

Winter. Can't wait to return to Book 2 and see what happens next in this lovely family saga.

★★★★★ Hooked from the first word!

I read this book in a day! I could not put it down! The story grips you right from the start! I've loved this series and as Ashley recommends, read them in order! I'm planning on re-reading this series as I've loved it!

★★★★★ All the elements for a great story

Just when you think Ashley has done her best work, she blows you away with an even better one. I loved this book. I couldn't put it down. The suspense and drama is magnificent. The love that shone like a golden thread throughout the book is done beautifully. I love it that true love wins in the end and that God is put in the centre of it. This series just keeps gettGARng better and better. I feel like I'm part of the family when I'm reading these books. The stories always leave me with a smile on my face. I love that all the characters as intertwined in some way or another. Well done Ashley!

"The Pretence" Series

Forget the Lies
Remember the Truth

Praise for "The Pretence"

★★★★★ Suspense and love story... true South African style story
I received an ARC copy of the book and was blown away by the story. The storyline is amazing and evolves quickly and keeps you guessing until the very end. True to Ashley's writing style there is always the Christian background and extra bit of evolvement in the believe department which leaves one inspired and warm and fuzzy inside. What I loved the most is that we revisited some of the characters from the Love South Africa series....it felt like visiting family. But the best is that you don't need to read the previous series to love this book. I can't wait for the follow up. Just love Ashley's writing style and how believable she makes all her books. She is by far my favourite writer. Love that she always writes the way we speak in South Africa and that you just want to read the whole book all at once.

★★★★★ Christian Romance and Suspense with a twist
Ashley Winter's storylines get better with each new book she delivers. I thought "Forget the Lies" was a good read, but "Remember the Truth" took it to a whole new level. I couldn't put my Kindle down until I had discovered the truth behind the elaborate plot. It is so refreshing to enjoy a good, clean suspense with a heart-warming love story thrown into the mix.

musings

from an african garden

7 days, 7 gardens,
7 glimpses of the Creator

Anna
JENSEN

MUSINGS FROM AN AFRICAN GARDEN

Acknowledgements

Thank you to **Craig**, **Caragh** and **Leal** for cheering me on along my writing journey. You keep it real!

Thank you to **Alison Theron** for all your reading, editing and creative assistance. I look forward to a long partnership of book perfecting.

Thank you to **Gwethlyn Meyer** for being a friend who holds me to account and keeps the creative energy high.

Thank you to **Sheena Carnie** for your encouragement and for being the best editor a girl could want.

And thank You, **Jesus**, for whispering Your command to 'Write what you see in a book' and for Your release of a whirlwind of words. Thank You for teaching me the delight of watching and listening.

To my Nan,

for planting in me the love of

all things garden.

Table of Contents

A Garden Story

I love gardens, especially public ones which are filled with exotic collections, hidden pathways and wide-open lawns. You know the ones where the trees have little labels fastened discreetly on to their trunks, declaring like a school name badge their genus and place of origin? My love of such places was birthed while growing up in Sheffield in the north of England. I went to a city school with no blade of grass in sight, just concrete playgrounds and paths. Playtime games often ended with grazed knees and tear-stained cheeks.

Over the road, however, were two magnificent parks where we would hold sports days and picnics. The closest, Endcliffe Park, dates back to 1885 and is a children's delight of sweeping grassy banks, a winding river and obligatory duck pond. Skipping across the busy roads in Noah-like two-by-two pairs, with our teachers standing in the middle of the road waving their arms enthusiastically in an attempt to halt the speeding cars, we would arrive giggling and breathless at the gate.

A bit further up the road are the Sheffield Botanical Gardens. Created in response to concerns that there weren't enough healthy green spaces being preserved in the ever-growing city, the Gardens were opened in 1836 after a competition for their design had been won by Robert Marnock. He incorporated the highly fashionable Gardenesque style, whereby each plant was displayed to perfection in its own setting rather than grouped with other trees or bushes of a similar variety as was common in other botanical collections. Small landscapes accentuated the beauty of each planting, with winding paths and grassy mounds adding further intrigue and interest.

At the time these were deemed the best gardens of the style in the whole of England. They were still magical to me 150 years later when, on school swimming days, we would once again pair up to cross busy roads and clump along pavements to the nearby swimming pool. Each week we passed the iron railings enclosing the botanical gardens, through which we would spy pathways disappearing through lush foliage leading to imagined worlds of fairies and unicorns. Occasionally we would take a special excursion to visit the Gardens, running around with shrieks of delight and waving crumpled worksheets aloft as we sought answers to the questions posed by our diligent teachers.

Those visits were great, but nowhere near as great as those undertaken with my Nan (grandmother) who lived near the bottom entrance to the Gardens. My sister and I would meet up with Nan and the three of us would go on adventures together, often with me passing on some vital piece of information gleaned from one of the aforementioned worksheets. We would stand in childish awe gazing at the great glass pavilions designed by Joseph Paxton, the man behind the magnificent Crystal Palace showcased in London at the Great Exhibition of 1851. One of them housed the aviary which Jane and I would plead to be allowed to enter so we could say hi to the red and blue macaw which sat on a perch just inside the door and greeted each visitor with a cheery 'Hello'. There was also a very talkative Indian mynah bird in one of the cages, the memory of which I now find particularly amusing as these birds are common visitors to our residential gardens here in Durban.

Once finished with the birds, we would then hare off into the rest of the garden, playing an exhausting game of hide and seek with each other, Nan in leisurely pursuit of the two of us. My personal favourite hiding place was through a section which, for some reason, was always fertilised with discarded hops retrieved from the nearby brewery. The sweet earthy smell wrinkled the nostrils but allowed for the quietest of footsteps!

And then there was the bear pit. Yes, Sheffield Botanical Gardens has a bear pit which was used to house a large black bear in the early days of the park. In later years it became the largest compost pit in Yorkshire, but as that is a little less romantic sounding, we'll keep it as the bear pit.

These early experiences of the delights a garden can bring have lived with me ever since. Whenever I explore a new town or city I inevitably find myself wandering not around the shopping malls or art galleries, but rather through the parks and gardens. I have stood under trees laden with enormous fruit bats in Sydney, browsed the Emperor's Gardens in Tokyo and passed through the imposing gates of Gorky Park in Russia. And in Africa? I have found a way to enjoy my not-so-English country garden, have snoozed under waving branches in Durban and been surprised by the arrival of a tortoise on the lawns in Cape Town. In each place I have felt the gentle touch of the Creator of the First Garden where Adam and Eve would walk in the cool of the day with God. I have heard His whispers and felt His presence as I've watched light and shade and history dance together in perfect harmony. I have glimpsed Him in many gardens, and I trust as you wander through these pages you will find much to muse upon as well.

Just a short note about language before we continue our sojourn into the world of garden spaces. I am a most English author, despite having lived in South Africa for many years; I therefore use British English phraseology and spelling rather than American, so please forgive me if anything isn't clear or isn't spelt as you might expect.

1

A Garden for the Soul

'For God alone, my soul waits in silence.'

Psalm 62:5

My parents have always been keen gardeners and it shows. I grew up playing on perfectly cut and tended green lawns under the shade of apple and pear trees. Weeping willows graced the boundary fence and planters and flowerbeds overflowed with every colour of the rainbow. Even my Nan's garden-less flat was a jungle of meticulously cared-for indoor houseplants. My particular favourite was one which filled and descended from its pot like a bright green wig. Sadly I don't seem to have inherited these gardening talents! I may love gardens, but I am most definitely not a gardener — I want instant and easy results and gardens just don't offer either.

Over the years spent living in South Africa I have tried to achieve my ideal garden numerous times — one full of flowers and a riot of colour to delight the eye all year round.

I have planted large earthenware pots full to glorious bursting with pansies and petunias and geraniums. I have tried tall standard roses and squat bushes and my all-time favourite, fuchsias; I adore their deep pink and purple flower drops, the buds of which make a satisfying 'pop' when squeezed between thumb and finger. Lavender bushes, herbs and salad vegetables have all been given a chance. They have all gone the same way, lost to all but memory. I am never sure whether I am over- or under-watering, whether the plant I am carefully nurturing needs hot full sun or a gentle cool shade. I have finally given up. Rather than the English country garden that my heart hankers after, we have now planted water-wise, rugged South African aloes and succulents.

Even though my garden is not necessarily all I had imagined it might be, it is still one of the most special spaces in the world to me. Over the years, especially since I started writing, I have spent many hours sitting in quiet contemplation in one or two favourite spots. I have an uninterrupted view of the Indian Ocean and the sound of crashing waves is a constant backing track to my thoughts. Birds are almost always overhead — the yellow-billed kites rising and soaring on unseen thermals of air, while visiting swallows flit and swoop as they catch lunch on the wing. Vervet monkeys regularly wander past, tightrope walkers on the fence who barely give me a glance as palm branches dance high above my head. It is here, amid the vibrancy of God's creation, that I am able to tell my soul to 'wait in silence for God alone'. The scurrying thoughts of my busyness and concerns are put to one side and instead I wait to hear what Jesus wants to whisper in my heart for that day, or for a particular article or poem.

It seems I am not alone in choosing a garden when seeking reflection or rest. On the night that Jesus was betrayed, He chose to spend the last hours before His arrest and crucifixion in the Garden of Gethsemane. The disciple John records that this was a place frequently visited by Jesus and his disciples (John 18:2). It was a place of familiarity and security, a refuge in a time of crisis. Jesus knew He would meet with His Father that night just as He had done on unrecorded occasions before. He knew He would be able to pour out His anguish and be sure of being heard, of being encouraged and strengthened in preparation for what lay ahead. The quiet of a garden was needed in that darkest hour.

If Jesus is our pattern, then perhaps we all need the quiet of a garden, a place we can go to that is free from the distractions and the doubts of the world. A place where our spirits can be replenished and our souls silenced while we wait for God alone to speak.

Do you have a 'garden' where you can sit and be quiet with your Father, where He can whisper truth and life and courage? It may not be an actual garden and it may not even be outside, but is there a place you can retreat to, where you can be assured of the comfort and guidance of your Father? If you do, why not head there now (if you're not already there) and allow the Holy Spirit to recharge and re-envision you.

Or maybe you don't have anywhere yet but feel desperate to get away from the noise and challenges of life for just a moment. Ask the Holy Spirit to show you, to bring somewhere to mind that He has prepared for you — perhaps in your own garden or yard, in a local park or even at an open window in your home. Hear the birds and feel the breeze and allow Jesus to gently speak.

Jesus, thank You that You understand the need for reflection and rest, that You also have been in the quiet of a garden so as to hear Your Father's heart. Thank You that You promise to lead me beside quiet waters and into pleasant places. I wait for You to remind me of old places or show me new ones, where I can still my soul to silently wait for You to speak.

2

A Garden of Beauty

'He has made everything beautiful in its time.'
Ecclesiastes 3:11

Once the decision was made to abandon the idea of a frothy English country garden and convert instead to a water-wise, easy to maintain South African version, we needed inspiration, guidance and plants. Thankfully I have a very good friend who has been a passionate advocate for just such a project and to whom I turned in my hour of need. Shirley has a burgeoning aloe garden of her own and has investigated and researched plant names, types and colours. She also knows the best places to buy them for the best price. On enquiring, she suggested Hackland Aloe Farm, located in the heart of the province's aloe country and just a little inland from Durban.

During the early weeks of the South African Covid-19 lockdown or stay-at-home orders our movements were highly restricted, meaning travel by car was limited to no more than a 5km (3 miles) radius from home. Thankfully after the first five weeks these restrictions were relaxed somewhat and it became possible to take trips slightly further afield. Shirley suggested we take one such trip, both as a way to meet up with each other after weeks of enforced isolation and also so we could seek out the best aloes on the market. We made our arrangements and packed a picnic lunch which she assured us we would be able to enjoy at the aloe farm itself.

As we drove the landscape changed from one of sub-tropical coastal forest, with its deep green banana bushes, paper-thin pink and white bougainvillaeas and leafy plane trees to a browner, drier view. Yet the winter dullness was punctuated and studded with the jewel-bright flowers of the aloes, emerging tall and proud above their stumpy succulent bodies, drawing the eye like the allure of candy at a fairground. Candelabras of blood-red vied for attention with delicate orange and vibrant yellow.

We turned off the main road and bumped and jiggled our way past tall palm trees and rustling sugar cane fields until we reached Hackland Farm. Shirley was already meandering through rows of plants, choosing which to take and which to leave. No neat garden centre pots and shelves here — these were real plants growing in real soil, each a transplanted offspring from the magnificence of the garden just beyond. This, the achievement of a lifetime of collecting and nurturing, and the place we would be enjoying our picnic, was a tumble of aloes, succulents and cacti, roses, trees, hidden pathways and secret benches.

We took our turn to examine the rows of plants on offer. It was hard to choose which would head home with us to start our garden. There were some with buttercup yellow flowers and others painted a delicate coral, while fiery reds rose like burning stakes. And then there were those which had no flowers but were instead decorated with needle-sharp spines all along their stems. It was all a bit overwhelming. We discussed our garden back home and tried to work out what would best fit where.

Finally we completed our purchases under the expert guidance of both Shirley and the owner, making sure our specimens had plenty of 'pups', or new shoots, for future growth. Then we spent the next few hours imagining the delights of what could be while enjoying our lunch. Bees hummed past us and brilliantly coloured sunbirds with their long hooked beaks gorged on nectar. Some plants towered above us while others were so tiny they were almost hidden from view. Each plant had been lovingly chosen, catalogued and nurtured, evidenced by the elaborate display all around us.

But here's the thing with aloes — they are dramatically attractive during the dry and relatively warm months of a South African winter, but really nothing special to look at during the summer. They are a tangle of thick, spiny leaves with little obvious appeal. Shunned by bee and bird alike, they offer nothing much by way of nutritional interest either. Summer is just not their time.

Now I hear the whisper of the Creator: sometimes it's not yet my time either. During those seasons when everyone else seems to be flowering and fruitful and I seem nothing more than a knot of unattractive leaves, my Father's promise that 'He has made everything beautiful in its time' (Ecclesiastes 3:11). It is amid the monotony of dusty winter that the aloe is the most striking; it is when night is at its darkest that a light is needed. Let me wait patiently for the season of the Lord and be made beautiful at a time that best suits His plans and purposes rather than my own.

Are you feeling frustrated or disappointed that nothing is in flower in your own life? Sit with Jesus and allow Him to reassure you of His perfect timing for every aspect of your life.

Father, thank You for the promise that You make everything beautiful in its own time. Thank You that You cause the aloe to bloom in the dryness of winter, reassuring me that Your timing is always perfect. Help me to wait patiently and diligently while You water and nourish me in preparation for the season to come. Use me to refresh the weary and nourish the hungry just as You use the winter blossoming of the aloe. Amen.

3

A Garden of Constancy

'Jesus Christ is the same yesterday and today and forever.'
Hebrews 13:8

In July 2014 my family and I took a long road trip from Durban on the east coast of South Africa to Harare in Zimbabwe to visit my sister-in-law and her family. This was a journey of 2,000km (1,243 miles) and took three days to complete; it was also one of the *funnest* trips we'd ever taken! We left home after church one Sunday, taking our time to reach the border. After staying overnight at a hot springs resort we set off early in the morning for the slow progression through the border post. And it certainly was slow, the computers crashing halfway through the process, resulting in a hot and tiring wait.

However once we made it through, our adventure in a new land could begin. We drove through valleys punctuated by the bare, upside-down looking branches of hundreds of baobab trees. We paused at every police road check into every small town, handing over our papers and having our vehicle assessed for any possible defects. We took a brief detour and visited the ancient site of Great Zimbabwe, an incredible rock fortress dating back to the 11th century. To climb the same steps as thousands of feet had done over millennia was a humbling experience.

We then made a mad dash to try and reach Harare before nightfall, bearing in mind that Zimbabwean roads overburdened with trucks are not the safest to negotiate in the dark. We reached the outskirts of the city in the dull orange glow of sunset, the smoke from cooking fires on either side of the road further obscuring our view and making driving a challenge. By the time we reached Leigh's home on the other side of town, stars were the only lights in the sky and we were dirty, hungry and tired. Her joyful welcome, a good meal and a good night's sleep soon revived us.

The next morning, while Leigh and her husband were at work, we headed out to explore Harare, this time in daylight. We drove along wide, dusty streets dwarfed by buildings familiar in every administrative capital around the world, their faded facades and broken windows testament to a country engulfed in chaos and division over decades. There was a sense that this is a city that has seen much, populated by a people who have felt much, and yet still they present their bravest faces and widest smiles to the outside world.

After driving around and getting our bearings a little, we made our way to the Harare Botanical Gardens for a bit of a wander, and hopefully a cup of tea or coffee while we were there. We parked under the cool shade of the trees guarding the entrance and made our way along the sandy pathways. Everything looked a little worn and neglected, with paint peeling off doors and window frames, and gate hinges rusty and hard to open. The thatched tea room seemed deserted at first but we were eventually able to get some attention and a drink. We sat at one of the concrete tables on the grass under a tree and looked around us.

There was a gentle rise of dry winter grass in front of us, edged on the far side by a collection of trees and shrubs, enticing in their size and stature. Cycads flourished and aloes blossomed. On the other side we glimpsed water — obviously a small lake of some sorts. Drinks finished, we headed off across the grass to see what treasures we would discover.

And treasures we did discover, but of an unexpected kind —those treasures when the Holy Spirit uses the natural, created world around us to highlight a truth about the Creator that we've maybe overlooked or forgotten. As we explored, I was struck by just how ancient some of those trees were. In some cases they had been growing in that one spot for literally hundreds of years. Other plantings had come and gone. Generations of people had passed by. Political leaders and systems had flourished and failed. Zimbabwe as a country has witnessed so much upheaval and experienced trials of an intensity that few of us will ever have to endure; even as I write the country is once more engulfed in violent confrontation. Yet here, amongst the solidity of these patient giants, there stands hope.

In the book of Hebrews Jesus is proclaimed to be 'the same yesterday, today and forever' (Hebrews 13:8); just like the trees towering above my head, He remains tall and strong and permanent regardless of the circumstances around us. In the midst of tumultuous change, insecurity and doubt, Jesus is the one constancy that I can turn to, that I can direct others to. He is an anchor that doesn't drag, a tower I can run into, the King above every other king that ever seeks his own throne.

Perhaps right now you feel as though uncertainty and change are the only two things that are certain. Take another look at what God has placed around you and be reminded that He does not change (Malachi 3:6).

 Jesus, thank You that You remain the same yesterday, today and tomorrow, and that You are seated on the throne regardless of any circumstance or situation I find myself in. Help me to keep my eyes fixed on You and Your unchanging presence and love during times I find stressful and difficult. And help me to point others to You when they don't know where to turn. Amen.

4

A Garden of the Senses

'For what can be known about God is plain to them, because God has shown it to them. For his invisible attributes, namely, his eternal power and divine nature, have been clearly perceived from the creation of the world in the things that have been made.'
Romans 1:19-20

It seems that in most of the places I've lived, I've been able to indulge in my love of public gardens and green spaces. Durban is no exception. Established in 1849, the Durban Botanic Gardens are the oldest survivors of their kind in the whole of Africa and were founded by Kew Gardens in London. Providing a nursery for newly discovered species which could then be taken back to London for display at Kew, the programme also worked on identifying plants with economic value which could be used to enrich the local community. One such crop which became the mainstay of agricultural production in the province was sugar cane, incidentally the industry my husband Craig now works in!

(As a little aside of personal interest, my Nan, she of the happy days of Sheffield garden adventures, grew up near Kew Gardens and it was one of her favourite spots to visit. She even has her initials carved in the bark of one of its most famous large trees! So maybe the love for all things botanical didn't start with me...)

I have spent many a happy hour or two at the Durban Botanic Gardens. They are cool, leafy and green, especially in the humidity of our east coast summers. The grass is thick and soft, the trees lofty and dense. There is a lake in the centre complete with lilies and pelicans; each summer, concerts are held on its grassy banks with mosquitoes playing their own unique accompaniment. During school holidays when the children were younger it was a regular destination for a picnic with friends.

The Gardens are separated into distinct sections, ranging from an award-winning orchid house to a fern dell and palm walkway. Hundred-year-old trees vie for attention with the oldest of plants, the cycads.

My personal favourite area is the sunken garden. Descending the few stone steps into this part of the Gardens is like entering another world — a bygone era of formal plantings and garden décor. Here there is a tranquillity, a seclusion that's lacking in other parts of the Gardens; the air rests still and heavy, flowers adorn the beds on either side of the pathway and ancient statues grace the four corners. Down a few more steps and along the centre runs a perfectly rectangular brick-edged pond, around which are planted more bright, seasonal blooms.

This is the place I love to linger, maybe to connect with my English country-garden heritage or maybe just to escape the noise and bustle of a city in full swing. Sheltered from the outside clamour by an ancient-looking face brick wall, even the birds sing softly and the bees buzz gently. It is in such a place that I can still the rushing of my thoughts and the anxieties of my heart, choosing to engage my senses and pay deliberate attention to my surroundings. Over the last few years the Holy Spirit has taught me the discipline and delight of noticing and absorbing and enjoying. I choose to attentively listen, deliberately trying to identify sounds, from the loudest traffic on the road outside to the smallest scrape of lizard feet on hot rock. I observantly look, noticing the ant on its journey or the ripple across the water. My fingers trace the roughness of stone.

We are wonderfully and fearfully created by our God. Every nerve-ending has a specific purpose, every cell a strategic design. And we are placed by Him in a sensory world filled with an orchestra of sound, a kaleidoscope of colour, a lavishness of smell and touch and taste. Paul tells the Romans that the 'invisible attributes of God, namely his eternal power and divine nature, are clearly perceived through all that He has made' (Romans 1:19-20). In the book 'The Practice of the Presence of God', Brother Lawrence tells how he learnt to focus on the presence of God at all times in the ordinary moments of everyday living. Like Paul, we will find that our God, our Heavenly Father, is neither distant nor silent; He is as close as a summer's breeze, as vocal as the morning's dawn chorus. It will take time and, yes, practice on my part to develop a habit of seeing and listening, but for the privilege of sitting with Jesus it will always be worth the effort.

How about you? Can you take a moment and engage your senses, choosing to notice God's created world around you right now? As you do, allow your mind to be quietened and your heart stilled, trusting that the Holy Spirit will reveal Jesus to you and fill you with His love and presence.

Father, thank You that You are not far off and distant but can be clearly perceived and known. Thank You that You have created me to be able to see and hear, to smell and taste and touch. Teach me how to really see, how to carefully listen, that I would become more aware of You and Your constant presence. Amen.

5

A Garden of Surprise

'And the angel said to them, "Fear not, for behold, I bring you good news
of great joy that will be for all the people."'

Luke 2:10

I think of all the botanical sites I've enjoyed few are quite as grand as
Kirstenbosch Gardens, situated on the slopes of the iconic Table
Mountain in Cape Town. Dating back to 1913, these gardens now boast
worldwide acclaim and are visited by over 75 000 people each year. I've
only been there on three or four occasions, but the first visit is perhaps
the most memorable. I was on holiday with my new husband, having
only arrived in the country six months earlier. My parents and sister had
flown over from the UK to experience my new home, and together we'd
travelled from Durban to Cape Town in search of sights.

Squeezing into our little white hire car, we drove from our
accommodation across town to Kirstenbosch. We found a shady parking
space and made our way to the glass-fronted entrance and visitors' centre
where we bought our tickets and browsed the art on display. The area
close to the main entrance is typical of botanic gardens everywhere —
there's a cafe, a book-and-souvenir shop, toilets and a myriad paths

heading off in different directions, luring the visitor into adventure and exploration.

 The most striking aspect to Kirstenbosch is its size and diversity of habitats, ranging from carefully curated lawns and flower beds through scrubby fynbos and wild proteas. We chose one of the paths in front of us and found ourselves in a beautiful open area of well-maintained, bright green grass, magnificently soaring trees and perfectly pruned bushes and shrubs. We wandered through this section at a leisurely pace, admiring the beauty of the flowers and marvelling at the carpet-like softness of the lawns beneath our feet.

Taking another path we found the terrain changing from the gentle space we'd just come from to one more densely planted and mysterious. We could hear water trickling nearby and smell the damp of the cool earth. Delicate ferns and ancient cycads stretched their leaves languidly across the path, relishing the shade in which they dwelt. Another turn and we were on a steep uphill climb through a glorious collection of proteas, South Africa's national flower. The ground was now dry and stony, no longer the domain of delicately waving leaves and dancing flowers, but rather of the rugged and strong. The sun was hot, the surrounding vegetation no longer tall enough to provide shade or shelter.

Had we continued, we would eventually have reached the summit of Table Mountain. However we were limited in both time and energy, and so turned and retraced our steps.

Once back to the lower slopes, we opted for a moment of rest on a bench overlooking the expanse of grass we'd walked across earlier. And then came the surprise. Out of the bushes behind us emerged two tortoises making their slow way down the hill. Up until that moment I had only ever thought of these creatures as pets that need their eyes cleaning at the end of winter hibernation. I'm not sure I'd even really considered them as wild animals, much less seen any in their natural habitat. And yet here were two such specimens clearly right at home and cared for by no-one but themselves. It was a moment of sufficient astonishment and revelation that it has remained lodged in my mind ever since.

Sometimes God arrests His people in ways that are as unexpected as a tortoise appearing from under a bush. Rainbows shatter a cloud-filled sky with promise of protection and provision (Genesis 9:13); angels announce miraculous conceptions and births (Luke 1) or appear in the pathway of warriors about to do battle (Joshua 5:14).

Each time, God's first words to His quaking child are 'Fear not'.

Fear not, for I have redeemed you.

Fear not, you are my beloved.

Fear not, be strong, stand firm.

Fear not, I have called you by name.

I can't say I've been visited by angels or been confounded by supernatural signs in the sky, but 'tortoises' in various guises still stop me in my tracks, forcing my attention heavenward. A tiny virus causing global chaos is one such tortoise. I had plans for 2020 — plans to travel and celebrate. Our daughter had 'final year of high school' plans. Everything has been postponed or cancelled or simply abandoned. I am left with a choice, to either sit in stupefied, frightened amazement at what has appeared in front of me, or to turn instead to Jesus and wait to hear his 'Fear not'.

How about you? Has a 'tortoise' shocked you by its sudden, unexpected appearance? Are you left wondering and questioning, or maybe just plain confused? May I encourage you to 'seek the Lord while He may be found, call upon Him while He is near ... "For my thoughts are not your thoughts, neither are your ways my ways," declares the Lord' (Isaiah 55:6, 8).

Thank You, Lord, that You are not surprised by circumstances or shaken by change. Thank You that You are the 'Ancient of Days', eternally seated on Your heavenly throne. Thank You that You use the unexpected and unusual to get my attention. Help me to turn to You right now and hear You say 'Fear not'. Thank You for Your immense love and care for me. Amen.

6

A Garden of Intent

'...having determined allotted periods and the boundaries of their dwelling place.'

Acts 17:26

I spent my teenage years living in Cornwall, in the far south west of England. It juts out far into the ocean, lending it an island-like quality. The southern beaches and rolling hills are more sheltered and serene than their wild northern counterparts where cliffs rise above crashing waves and frothing surf. Secluded coves whisper of smugglers and pirates, and the crumbling remains of tin mine engine-houses dot the landscape, punctuation marks of history telling long forgotten stories. The inland moors featured in Daphne du Maurier's 'Jamaica Inn' are rugged and inhospitable, often shrouded in mist and fog, whereas lower farming regions are the lush and green homes of cows and sheep.

My parents still live in Cornwall and so it's a regular stop on our itinerary when we head back to the UK for holidays. Usually we relax at home, taking long walks along windy cliff tops or drinking tea while chatting. One year, by way of a change, we decided to visit a newly-opened tourist attraction — The Eden Project.

The Eden Project began life in 1995 as an end-of-commercial-life china clay pit and a dream in the heart of a gardener, Sir Tim Smit.

Similar to the thinking behind the botanical gardens of previous generations, the vision was to create a spectacular showcase of the world's most important plants while simultaneously developing a base for scientific research. After contemplating various architectural options, an innovative design featuring two large bubbles was settled upon, and the Eden biomes were born

By the time we visited in around 2003, the site had become reasonably established and was a top visitor destination in Cornwall. It opened in March 2001, and by June of the same year over 1 million people had paid their entrance fees and been awed at what lay beyond the car park.

It really is a surreal sight. A steep walkway descends from the entrance area down into the bottom of the old pit where the biomes rest like giant bubble-wrap lumps just waiting to be popped. Each bubble has its own unique climate — one tropical and the other Mediterranean. On our visit we first turned left into the warmth of the tropical dome, now home to the largest indoor rainforest in the world.

We peeled off layers of clothing as we entered, enjoying the familiarity of warm humidity while quietly chuckling at those around us who were complaining about the heat and the damp. This was Durban on a hot summer's day. As we followed a well-marked route through the undergrowth, we were amused to see so many plants that grow almost like weeds in our garden back home. Granted, these were bigger and more spectacular, but they were the same plants nonetheless. On the one hand we were disappointed to not discover anything particularly new or exciting, but on the other we were delighted to show our family just a little of our life back in South Africa.

After a reasonable time spent pottering in the jungle we retraced our steps and entered the Mediterranean Biome opposite. This was distinctly underwhelming given the abundance of greenery next door; here the plants were small and stunted, growth slow in the simulated arid climes of the Mediterranean. As we shuffled unappreciatively past rocky flower beds and spiky cacti, we were surprised to encounter an entire section dedicated to the marvel that is South African fynbos — the proteas and heathers found around Cape Town and surrounds. The specimens in residence in Cornwall were small, not yet fully established or thriving in their new environment. And yet they were there — ambassadors of a distant land planted in foreign soil, heralds of far-off riches. Not accidental, but deliberately chosen.

Everything contained within the two indoor biomes at the Eden Project is there for a purpose, and has been picked and planted, cultivated and nurtured with care. I am reminded of Paul's speech at the Areopagus in Athens: 'The God who made the world and everything in it, being Lord of heaven and earth...himself gives to all mankind life and breath and everything. And he made from one man every nation of mankind to live on all the face of the earth, having determined allotted periods and the boundaries of their dwelling place' (Acts 17:24-26).

Just as the Eden Project's horticulturists and botanists choose with intent what plant needs to be placed when and where; just as sophisticated technology controls the details of temperature and humidity to create the perfect environment, so too does our Father in Heaven intimately concern himself with when and where we live, with exact times and set places. Like the fynbos, we are ambassadors of another King, heralds of a different Kingdom (2 Corinthians 5:20).

Do you sometimes feel out of place, undernourished and weak? Be assured that you are planted in exactly the place that God wants you to be in at this given moment. He will water you, He will feed you, He will nurture and grow you until you become the dazzling display of His goodness you are intended to be.

Father, thank You that You have set times and places for me to be planted where I will thrive and display Your goodness to the world around me. Thank You that where I am right now is because of You, even if at times I find it hard or uncomfortable. Help me not to look at outward circumstances but rather to seek You for Your watering and nurturing. Amen.

7

A Garden of Work

'The Lord God took the man and put him in the Garden of Eden to work
it and keep it.'
Genesis 2:15

One of the things I enjoy doing after dropping the children off at
school for the day is to meet a friend and wander the streets of the suburb
of Durban where she lives. It is an old, established part of town, with
wide streets, huge properties and magnificent gardens. As we walk and
talk, I glimpse snatches of these gardens through fences and gates. They
range in style from English countryside to South African indigenous and
everything in between. Some have pools and ponds, others twisting paths
and paved seating areas. One thing they all have in common — I never
see anyone in them, enjoying them.

This saddens me. A garden should be enjoyed, lived in, utilised. I
know just such a garden, located in a small hamlet in the southernmost
corner of Eswatini (Swaziland). This is a very 'British' garden; not owing
to its wild profusion of delicate flowers and bowling-green lawns, but
because it is owned and worked by a Swazi pastor friend of ours whose
name is British!

We first met British when he visited our church in South Africa. After a Sunday service complete with the full-voiced, animated preaching British employs so well, we gathered together for lunch. As we chatted and got to know one another better, a plot was hatched to take a team up to the church British was leading in Eswatini. Over the coming weeks we made all the necessary preparations, making sure we collected all the items British wanted us to take with us — mainly books that he could use in the Bible school he ran at church.

The day of the expedition dawned and we travelled north, eventually reaching the border around midday. Once through Customs we continued on our way until we arrived at our rendezvous point with British — a petrol station on the outskirts of the town of Hlatikulu. After a bit of a wait British arrived and we followed him the rest of the way to his home and church. The road climbed steeply out of Hlatikulu, winding through villages preceded by the worst speed humps I've ever seen. The views were spectacular, with deep valleys intersecting the tree-crowned hill tops. Homesteads lay to either side of the road — traditional round houses and modern rectangular blocks all painted alike in bright blues, greens and white. Children returning from school, smart in their uniforms, made their noisy, boisterous way home. Goats and cows risked their lives trying to reach the juiciest grasses at the edge of the highway.

We finally reached our destination, beating the setting sun by minutes only. We were staying at a farm close to where British lived, his own home too small to accommodate us. After a specially prepared meal of chicken, rice and pickled beetroot, we flopped with gratitude into bed.

We were awoken bright and early the next day by the family rooster, declaring indignantly that we really had been in bed too long! We boiled a pan of water on the stove, made tea and ate breakfast. While we waited for British to collect us, we explored our home of the next few days. The children were intrigued by the little houses woven together from sticks and placed high above the ground for the chickens to roost in at night, and they chased young bleating goats around their dusty enclosure. Soon British arrived and we went with him a little further along the road to his home and the church building.

British and his wife, Sisakela, welcomed us to their home with hugs and smiles. We were ushered to stools placed in the cool shade and given juice to drink. As we looked around we marvelled at the enormous size of the cabbages in their garden. This was no ornamental garden designed for rest and relaxation, but rather a garden to be worked, a garden from which food and sustenance was demanded.

In the account of creation in Genesis chapter 2, God 'took the man and put him in the Garden of Eden to work it and keep it' (Genesis 2:15). The Garden of Eden was to be a place of provision and blessing, a place where Adam could enjoy the product of his labours. Our Heavenly Father is a busy, creative, productive God, and as we are made in his image, we are to be likewise. In his letter to the Ephesians, Paul writes that 'we are [God's] workmanship, created in Christ Jesus for good works, which God prepared beforehand, that we should walk in them' (Ephesians 2:10). A productive garden needs attention; it needs to be worked and tended to if it is to bear the fruit required of it. So does the garden of my heart if I am to fulfil all that God has promised. I need to be regularly washed and watered by the Word, kept soft by the gentle whisper of the Holy Spirit.

Do you need to be refreshed and ploughed, made ready for new seeds to be planted? Or are you feeling ready for harvest? Come before the best Gardener now and allow Him to do His work.

Father, thank You that You created the First Garden, and that You planned for it to be fruitful and productive. Thank You that You have planned the same for the garden of my life, and have created in advance good works for me to do. I invite You to come and work in Your garden, to weed and water, to sow and reap. Amen.

About the Author

I'm a British expat who has lived in South Africa for a little over twenty years. My husband and I live with our two teenage children on the east coast, a few miles north of the city of Durban. We overlook the Indian Ocean where we have the privilege of watching dolphins and whales at play.

My first book 'The Outskirts of His Glory' was published in May 2019. The book is a Christian devotional and poetry collection exploring the many surprising ways that God can speak to us through His creation. I have drawn on my travels in and around South Africa, as well as further afield, to hopefully inspire each of us to slow down and perhaps listen more carefully to the 'whispers of His ways' (Job 26:14) that are all around us.

Since publishing 'Outskirts', I have had the privilege of speaking at a number of local churches and even have a weekly slot on a Christian radio station. I have also continued writing by contributing to a variety of blogs and online writing communities as well as developing my own website and blog.

Want to know more? You can find me at

Website: www.annajensen.co.uk

I send out a more-or-less monthly newsletter which you can subscribe to if you'd like to find out what's happening in the world of Anna! It includes my latest blog post about whatever God is saying and doing in my life at any given moment; there are also book reviews, guest posts and promos. It's free and you can unsubscribe whenever you like. Sign up through my website.

Email: I'd love to hear from you too. You can email me at hello@annajensen.co.za

More from Anna

If you enjoyed this devotional from Anna, you might like to check out her other books. Click on the image to go the Amazon sales pages, or you can buy direct from Anna's website www.annajensen.co.uk

The Outskirts of His Glory

Join Anna Jensen and her family as they travel to seek out and experience the odd and unexpected of God's creation.

Captivated by the Creator (paperback only)

Be inspired afresh by the voice of the Creator through the beauty of His creation. Be guided by Anna Jensen as she describes her own journey of discovery through articles and poems. This beautiful journal contains pictures for you to colour and space for your own thoughts and prayers.

Twenty Years an Expat

Read about Anna's experiences as she leaves her native land and learns to embrace the different and the new as she settled in South Africa. At times funny, at others poignant, the one constant is God's love and purpose for Anna in all she experiences.

Poetry and Prayer

Anna started writing poems in earnest just a few years ago...Her poetry will always begin and end with Jesus. He is the master craftsman, the great author, The Word. In this way, each poem is indeed a prayer — of thanksgiving, of worship, of truth — whispered in her innermost parts. As you read both the poems, and the thinking behind them, it is her prayer that Jesus would woo you afresh with His presence.

Poems from an African garden

A poem is like a garden bench; it offers a moment for pause and contemplation, an opportunity to think a little deeper and go beyond the simple. Here, Anna Jensen places a 'bench' in each of seven African gardens, offering space into which the Creator God can whisper. This book can be found in this set of books.

Life is Good

7 DAYS OF APPRECIATING LIFE'S GIFTS

Yvonne Tippins

LIFE IS GOOD

Acknowledgements

Thank you to Sabine Cox for the use of her beautiful artwork for my front cover. All other artwork is my own.

Thank you to Shirley Corder for all she has done to put this initiative together.

Dedicated to all those who make my life good...
especially to Mark and Laura who share my challenges and adventures daily.

Life is Good has been written in British English.

Table of Contents

Day 1

Perspective: It is not what we see that matters but how we choose to look at things.

"Whatever is true, whatever is noble, whatever is right, whatever is pure, whatever is lovely, whatever is admirable if anything is excellent or praiseworthy think about such things."
(Philippians 4:8)

I remember seeing a cartoon depicting two guys travelling in a bus along a winding mountain road. To the right of the bus there was a breath-taking vista of rolling hills and a verdant green valley. To the left of the bus there was a cliff face, a solid mass of grey rock limiting any view at all.

The guy on the right (let's call him Ray Sunny) looked animated and excited and appeared to be happily enjoying his journey while the guy on the left (let's call him Jim Grim), looked bored, glum and disinterested. These were two travellers on the same journey, but their individual perspectives were clearly influencing their perception of their experience and hence their emotional reaction to the trip.

When I am out and about and watching the people around me, I love to build stories around how they seem to be experiencing their day. In this case, I imagine both Ray and Jim were on their way to enjoy a holiday at the sea. Ray got up in the morning feeling eager and excited about the day ahead. He was enjoying taking in all the sights as they travelled along. Jim, on the other hand, got up feeling disgruntled because he would have to endure a long bus trip to get to his destination. To add insult to injury he had also been given a bad seat on the bus where he only had a cliff face to look at.

There are several things Jim could have done differently to have had a better experience. He could have started his day with a more positive outlook, appreciative that he was going on a journey to enjoy a lovely holiday at the sea. He could have tried to change his seat on the bus so he had a better view, or he could have enjoyed the current perspective and waited for the view to change. He probably wouldn't have had to look at the cliff face for the entire journey. I imagine that as the bus meandered along, Ray would also have his turn to look at the cliff, but he would still be smiling happily as he enjoyed the new perspective.

This story is a lot like our lives. Often, we allow our current perspective or circumstances to cloud our perceptions and experiences of events and this also influences our emotional reactions. We are all on the same journey called life, but we all face different circumstances at different times. Some, like Ray, are going through good times. Others, like Jim, are experiencing hardship.

As we go through life, things are constantly changing and a bad day or a period of lows doesn't mean we are having a bad life. We, like Jim, could do things differently and wake up each day with a positive outlook, appreciative of what we have rather than focussing on what we don't have.

We need to look at the roses rather than the thorns. When things are tough, we could focus on either finding ways to change the circumstances we find ourselves in, or we could take time to breathe as we wait for things to change. They inevitably do.

Happy people are not those who have perfect lives, they are those who appreciate the life they have and make the best of it. They are those who find joy in the journey.

I had a lovely friend who recently passed away but I will always remember how, when she walked into a room, she always brightened the atmosphere with the Bible verse from Psalm 118:24: "This is the day that the Lord has made, we will rejoice and be glad in it". Her life, I am sure, was not always perfect, but she lived every day with a grateful heart, rejoicing in the Lord... and it was infectious.

Although it can sometimes be difficult, try to be more like Ray and never let a day go by without seeing what is good, feeling the good within you, praising, being grateful and appreciating every aspect of the journey of life.

Enjoy the Journey – Dream Big

Live Simply – Be Grateful

Be Authentic

SMILE

Day 2
Expectancy: Look forward to new life experiences with awe and wonder.

"The whole earth is filled with awe at your wonders; where morning dawns, where evening fades, you call forth songs of joy."
(Psalm 65:8)

It was New Year's Eve 2012, and we were on a flight homeward bound after a 3-week holiday in the UK and Europe. We had woken early in our hotel in Paris near to the airport, flown to Amsterdam for our connecting flight, and run through Schiphol Airport to make it in time for our flight back to South Africa. We then spent several hours on the plane to get home.

It had been a long day and we felt deflated because our holiday was over. I had even forgotten it was New Year's Eve and we were about to take on an exciting new year. As we were getting ready to disembark, a little boy in the row in front of us had just woken up. His dad was helping him fetch his bag from the overhead compartment and I overheard him say excitedly to his dad, "Dad we're in Africa! We're in the jungle. We're on another planet".

This little child's amazing sense of awe and wonder at what he expected to experience in South Africa touched me deeply. He was unconcerned about the potential for uncertainty and danger on this "new planet". He had no idea of what it would be like out there when he was off the plane, but he saw it as a wonderful adventure.

He also knew his father was by his side and would protect and guide him as he explored this "new planet".

As we grow older, we tend to take things for granted instead of looking at each new experience as an adventure and a gift. Life is a gift, a gift to appreciate, cherish and enjoy with excitement and expectancy. Often, we allow the uncertainty that comes with new experiences to taint the enjoyment of the gift instead of looking at it with the awe and wonder of a child. Things don't always turn out as we expect they will. We do need some awareness of the potential dangers which accompany new experiences. But we don't need to start the journey expecting the worst. Life can be an adventure, full of ups and downs. We need to appreciate and enjoy the journey with gratitude.

Among many other promises, God assures us in His word that although there may be mountains and storms in our way in life, He will always be with us as we climb the mountains and overcome the storms. Let gratitude be your umbrella during the storms.

Your mindset and attitude can have an immensely powerful effect on your life. By developing an attitude of positive, cheerful, and eager expectancy we can live in anticipation of God's many blessings and we can trust He will help us to overcome any difficulty along the way. God is so good. He wants your life to be a wonderful adventure, but you must be ready to let Him move, and be excited to take on the challenges.

Always believe something wonderful is about to happen and as it says in 1 Timothy 6:17 …"Fix your hope on God, the one who richly provides everything for our enjoyment."

When you look at life through the eyes of gratitude with the awe and wonder of a child, knowing our heavenly Father will be with us through it all, the whole world becomes a magical and amazing place.

Believe that Something

Wonderful is

About to Happen...

Day 3

Hindsight:Trials are often blessings in disguise.

"Consider it pure joy, my brothers and sisters, whenever you face trials of many kinds, because you know that the testing of your faith produces perseverance."

(James 1: 2-3)

My daughter is a University lecturer and often, while she is marking assignments, we have a good laugh at the amusing things the students write. One of her students recently made a comment in an assignment about "Heinzsight" which you can imagine led to lots of amusing retorts. One being, "Heinzsight is the ability to realise you didn't need all those tins of baked beans to get through the 2020 lockdown after all."

2019 was a tough year for us as a family. We had planned a visit to friends in Australia and shortly before we were due to fly out my husband's work contract ended. We enjoyed our trip but when we returned, we faced 9 months of difficult times as he tried to find work. By the grace of God, we somehow managed to get through it all as a family. Then, just as things were getting back to normal, 2020 arrived with all its many challenges.

In hindsight, 2019 was a walk in the park compared to what we have already experienced in the first 6 months of 2020 but our experiences in 2019 went a long way to prepare us to deal with what was to come. 2019 also helped me to learn to persevere and trust in God's perfect plan and provision in what has been a very uncertain and troubling year for the whole world.

I remember a quote that said "Never regret a day in your life. Good days give you happiness, bad days give you experience, the worst days give you lessons, and the best days give you memories". Oscar Wilde said, "What seem to us as bitter trials are often blessings in disguise". The word of God also tells us that life is full of trials and suffering but we can trust God to bring us through these times. Trust in God's plan for your life. *"For I know the plans I have for you"*, declares the Lord, *"Plans to prosper you and not to harm you, plans to give you hope and a future"* (Jeremiah 29:11). It's hard to be grateful for the "not so good" things we experience in life but often these experiences are part of God's greater plan to prepare us for what lies ahead. We often go through a season in our lives for a reason and only when we look back, do we see His perfect plan unfolding. Try to look for the hidden blessing in every day, even during tough times.

There is a good reason why the rear-view mirrors in your car are so much smaller than the windscreen. The mirrors allow you to check and remain aware of where you have come from to avoid pitfalls, but the windscreen gives you a wide view of the direction you are going in and all the wonderful things ahead and around you.

Be grateful for what the past has taught you, find joy in the present, and enthusiastically prepare for a positive future. Hindsight, or "Heinzsight", is important but it is merely preparing us for the adventures and sometimes challenges that lie ahead.

In Hindsight,

Trials are often

Blessings in

Disguise...

Day 4

Simple things: Practising gratitude for the small, everyday things.

"The kingdom of heaven is like a mustard seed, which a man took and planted in his field. Though it is the smallest of all seeds, yet when it grows, it is the largest of garden plants and becomes a tree, so that the birds come and perch in its branches."

(Matthew 13:31-32)

I have just spent the last three months, while in various stages of lockdown in South Africa to contain the spread of COVID-19 caused by the novel coronavirus, making a quilted wall-hanging for a competition. When asked to submit an entry, I wondered about a theme for the wall hanging and thought about what was nurturing me through this unprecedented and uncertain period of life. I decided that it is the small things, the everyday things and the seemingly insignificant things we take for granted which keep me moving forward. I named my entry "The Simple things" and it was made up of 19 small 5 inch squares, depicting those aspects of life that bring me joy in uncertain times. My home, family, friends and symbols of love and spirituality. Images of garden, birds, pets, flowers, pots of tea, cupcakes and yummy treats all adorn my wall hanging. I found the process of focusing on, and being grateful for, all these little things quite therapeutic in dealing with what is going on in the big world out there. I realised that being thankful and appreciating all these little things is what creates a full and joyous life.

I love this quote by Ann Voskamp, "Joy is the realest reality, the fullest life, and joy is always given, never grasped. God gives gifts and I give thanks and I unwrap the gift given: joy."

It's the little things that make up the whole. If you miss the small things, you miss the bigger picture, the gift of God's endless love for us. There is amazing power in small things. One merely has to consider the impact of the tiny bee on the food supply of the whole of humanity to see this power. Small things matter to God and He often uses small things to accomplish big plans. Joseph in the Bible was one little kid whom God used to preserve the Israelite nation and change the course of history. David was just a little shepherd boy but he faithfully served God and became a great warrior and king. The story of Jesus also began with a tiny baby in a manger in a little town, and He grew up to influence history and save the whole world. As small and insignificant as we are, if we walk in faith and obedience to God, we too can be used to achieve God's bigger purposes.

Appreciate all the small things that we can contribute to God's kingdom. *Rejoice always, pray continually, give thanks in all circumstances; for this is God's will for you in Christ Jesus"* (Thessalonians 5:16-18).

These are all simple things that we can do. Always remember that everything you have and everything you do, both big and small, is because of the grace of our loving God. In uncertain times, be grateful for the little things and stitch them into your life.

Appreciate the

Simple

Things

Day 5
Renewal: Start each day with a grateful heart.

"Create in me a pure heart, O God, and renew a steadfast spirit within me."

(Psalm 51:10)

Just before the beginning of the hard lockdown to control the spread of COVID-19 here in South Africa, a special friend of mine arrived on my doorstep with a beautiful bunch of magnificent sunflowers grown on their farm. It was such a wonderful and unexpected blessing for me when things were looking bleak. They brought me an amazing sense of joy.

When we receive unexpected gifts we always appreciate them with joy but if my friend brought me sunflowers every week, I might start to get used to them and take them for granted, that I would always have sunflowers to brighten my home. Eventually, if she stopped bringing sunflowers for whatever reason, I might begin to feel hurt and sad or even angry at her because I now feel entitled to my weekly sunflowers. Entitlement is the exact opposite of gratitude and when I begin to feel entitled, my gratitude and joy shrinks in proportion.

Unfortunately, the world often cultivates a sense of entitlement by making us believe we deserve what we have, we are amazing and people are lucky to have us. Instead, we need to recognise everything we have and all we are is actually a gift and a privilege. Every day we open our eyes and take another breath is a gift.

Gratitude is an attitude of appreciation we choose. A mindset where we acknowledge that, in fact, everything we have is an unearned and unexpected blessing, a surprise bunch of sunflowers.

Research has shown that by being grateful we become open to more possibilities and we experience more happiness and higher levels of energy and motivation. Being grateful also builds and sustains better relationships and helps us to get through life's many difficulties.

In my kitchen I have a picture frame with a special photo of my husband and myself enjoying a beautiful sunset in a place where we were happy and relaxed. On the frame, I have an inscription saying, "Start each day with a grateful heart". It reminds me each day as I go into the kitchen to renew my choice. A happy life is one where you choose each day to be grateful and appreciate what you have, where you live each day with a grateful heart. It is a renewable energy source for every day. It's up to you to make the choice.

A simple way to start developing a sense of gratitude rather than entitlement is to take a few moments each day to think of, meditate or pray about, and perhaps even write in a journal, three things for which you are grateful.

Just the other day, I was sorting the family laundry and feeling very disgruntled that I had to endure this chore, when I picked up my husband's "not so fresh" socks. Suddenly, I thought how lucky I am to have these people in my life whom I can serve in this way. How grateful I am to have a loving husband and a beautiful daughter to do life with. Suddenly my annoyance turned to peace and joy.

I remember reading a simple prayer which summed it all up and it went something like this... "Thank you Lord for the wonderful life I have and the people I do life with. Please bless us each day with peace and joy." Amen. The Bible reminds us to *"Rejoice in hope, be patient in trouble and be constant in prayer"* (Romans 12:12).

Psychology has also shown that if we move through each day with an open awareness of the many good things around us, we correct the brain's built-in negativity bias. It rewires our brains to look for positive possibilities rather than problems and generally improves our happiness and well-being.

We receive unexpected and unearned gifts from God each day of our lives. God is always steadfast and faithful, and His mercies are new every morning (Lamentations 3:22-23). *Our role is to choose to be grateful each day.*

His Mercies
Are
New Every Day

Day 6
Authenticity: Embracing who you were created to be.

"I praise you because I am fearfully and wonderfully made; Your works are wonderful; I know that full well."
(Psalm 139:14)

I hate it that I am so imperfect. As one of life's unbearable perfectionists, I have always beaten myself up and become irritated by imperfection. I feel I should be something I am not.

We all have a little voice in our heads, our "inner critic", that little voice which tells you, "you are not good enough", "no one will like you", "you are not beautiful", "you are too fat or too skinny", "you will never amount to anything", "you are not clever enough", "you are too old or too young", "you have failed", "what will people think of me" or my favourite, "you are not qualified". Very often that inner critic steals our joy, creates limiting beliefs about who we are and what we can do and reduces our sense of self-worth. Unfortunately, in life, my biggest struggle has been with comparison and comparison is the thief of joy.

When you look in the mirror and tell yourself you are average or inadequate or not enough, you are simply not seeing yourself as God sees you. He has created each one of us on this earth in a unique and special way. Out of the billions of people in the world there is no one exactly like you. You are rare and valuable in God's eyes.

In the verse above, David is praising God that he is *fearfully and wonderfully made*. He is in awe of the greatness of God. He is appreciative of who God has made him. He recognises he is great only because of the greatness of God. Every individual is God's masterpiece and we are made in His image. When that nasty little inner voice criticises us, we are not only criticising ourselves but also criticising the God who made us and designed us exactly the way He wanted us to be. This world needs the person whom you were made to be.

I recently read a quote, "*Perfectionism is the most paralysing form of self-abuse*". Instead of bringing out the best in us, it makes us focus on the worst in ourselves, the inadequacies and the part that tells us that nothing we are, and nothing we do, will ever be good enough. But if I am grateful for who I am and who God has created me to be, I am able to see I am enough. Every experience I have had up to now has shaped me into the person I am today and that is who I am supposed to be. It frees us up to grow and to fulfil the purpose God has for our lives. Just be yourself, the perfectly imperfect, quirky, beautiful, and unique individual you were created to be.

Make a conscious choice to change the way you see yourself and the language you use to describe yourself. Proactively seek out ways to find joy and fulfilment, respect yourself and the unique character and abilities God gave you. Test your limits by taking brave action out of your comfort zone to find out what you can do. If you have always believed you are not creative, try to do something that tests your creativity. Even if it doesn't turn out perfectly, look at what you have learnt and how you have progressed. Appreciate the steps you are taking to see yourself as capable, good enough, valuable and amazing. Be grateful for who you are and be authentically the *you* that only you were meant to be.

The only person who can be ME is ME! Perfectly, imperfect ME. Be grateful for being you. Use the talents you have been given and forget about being perfect, just be authentic. The world would be incredibly quiet if the only birds to sing were those that sang the most perfectly and beautifully.

Fearfully and Wonderfully Made...

Day 7:
Connection: Appreciation of others

"Therefore encourage one another and build each other up, just as in fact you are doing."
(1 Thessalonians 5:11)

We are not alone in this world, although lately we have been through a time when isolation has made many people feel alone. I believe in the value of a smile. When we see someone who is clearly having a tough day, often just a simple smile from a stranger can make them feel a whole lot better about life. A simple smile is a bit like an unexpected gift.

We have a car guard at our local shopping centre whom my daughter and I have nicknamed "Smiley". No matter what he has been through, he always greets everyone he meets with a warm and welcoming smile. On many occasions, he has made me realise how "life is actually so very good" no matter what the circumstances. I have missed those smiles as we all hide behind our COVID masks, but I can see his eyes and I know he is still smiling. Coincidentally, he has a mask with a donkey face on it with a huge grin. This makes me smile.

Every individual you meet in life is also a unique individual, created by God for a purpose. Often that purpose is linked in some way and influences the lives of those around them. Life is a complex set of interconnections. In life we meet many people and each one has some role to play in our lives. Some are there to test us, some are there to teach us something, some will use us, and some will love us. But then there will be those who bring out the best in us, who encourage us and make us realise how worthwhile life is. So worthwhile. We should be grateful for all these people but especially for those who give meaning to our lives.

A simple thank you for the way someone's friendship has helped you grow, grounded you, lifted your spirits or brightened your day, can go a long way to connecting us and making the world a far better place.

Brené Brown speaks about connection as "The energy that exists between people when they feel seen, heard and valued; when they can give and receive without judgement and when they derive sustenance and strength from the relationship." And according to Margaret Wheatley, "When we seek connection, we restore the world to wholeness. Our seemingly separate lives become meaningful as we discover how absolutely necessary we are to each other".

I have learnt an important lesson over time: it is not what I have in my life, but who I share my life with that makes all the difference. I cherish those who selflessly support me, make me smile, bring me joy, show me kindness, and help me to grow and give my life purpose. These people are a special gift.

When you see something beautiful in someone, connect with them, don't hesitate to tell them. It may take you a moment to do but it could change their whole life, knowing that they are appreciated. A simple smile (even behind our masks) can be encouraging and make someone's day.

Stay Close

to Those Who

Make You Feel

Like Sunshine...

About the Author

Yvonne is a South African author living in Vereeniging alongside the Suikerbos River with her husband, Mark and only daughter (Author and English Lecturer), Laura.

She is qualified in the field of Psychology and works as a Consultant in the Development of people. She loves to see people growing and thriving and making the most of their "God given" potential.

Yvonne has only recently begun on the journey of writing as another way to inspire and encourage others. She is also a keen artist, crafter, photographer and publisher and believes in the value of using creativity for growth and healing. Other published work so far includes; "I Love My Job - Finding fulfilling work"

Our lives are full of many ups and downs. This little booklet contains 7 days of reflection on what can make life good. I hope it encourages and inspires you to appreciate each day on your life journey with awe and wonder and a grateful heart.

Yvonne

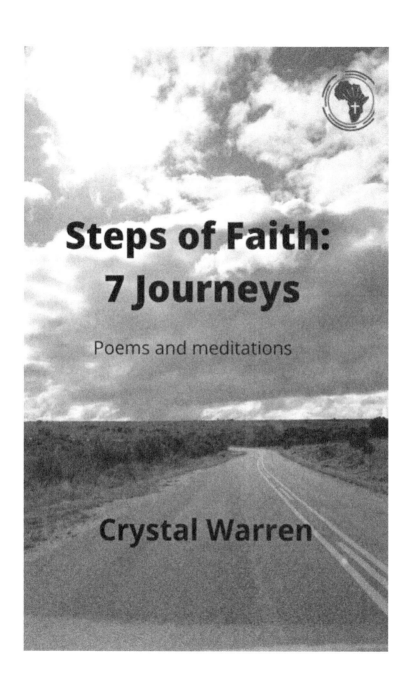

Steps of Faith: 7 Journeys

Poems and meditations

Crystal Warren

STEPS OF FAITH

Versions of some of these poems have appeared in my previous collections: *Predictive Text* (Modjaji Press, 2019) and *Bodies of Glass* (Aerial Publishing, 2004) and the journals *Aerial* and *Journeyings*.

Cover photograph by Crystal Warren.

This booklet follows British English.

Table of Contents

Introduction

I live in a small town in the Eastern Cape of South Africa. One must travel an hour and a half to Port Elizabeth or two hours to East London to catch an airplane, see a medical specialist, watch a film, or anything else that requires a city. I grew up in Port Elizabeth and still have family there so I visit frequently. As a child we regularly visited my grandparents who lived near East London. So, I have spent a lot of time travelling these roads. My job requires me to travel a lot as well, either flying from Port Elizabeth or driving to Cradock and other Eastern Cape Towns.

Long car rides are a good time to think, to reflect (especially if you get carsick and can't read in the car). A lot of my poems have been composed in cars, and a fair number focus on the road between Port Elizabeth and Makhanda (formerly Grahamstown). Another activity conducive to poetry production is walking. Many poems slowly develop while I am walking to and from work. There is something about the rhythm of the steps, the silence, the time to notice what is around that can be almost meditative.

The road also helps us to reflect on our spiritual journey. Sometimes we are driving for hours, at other times walking slowly, one step at a time. We might have maps and guides, but the path ahead is unknown and each step, each turn of the tyres, is an act of faith until we reach our final destination.

These poems about journeys, about walking or driving, will hopefully help you think about where you are on your journey with God.

1

Exodus

*"By day the LORD went ahead of them in a pillar of cloud to guide them
on their way and by night in a pillar of fire to give them light, so that
they could travel by day or night. Neither the pillar of cloud by day nor
the pillar of fire by night left its place in front of the people."*
(Exodus 13:21-22)

the storm is breaking
dark clouds cover the sky

leading me through the desert
the flame flickers and dies

smoke rising to meet the rain

Sometimes things are not as they seem. Joseph was sold into slavery
in Egypt and suffered at first. But God used him to save his family. In
time the refuge of Egypt became a prison, with the people of Israel
enslaved. Exodus tells the story of how God lead them out of slavery and
eventually into the promised land. But it was a long journey, forty years

154

of wandering through the wilderness. Some of the people complained, claiming that they were happier in Egypt and would now die. Yet God was with them all the way, providing protection, food and water, and giving them guides of clouds and flames.

Even when it seems that our journey is taking us through a dark and desolate place, we can trust that God is with us, leading us on. If the flame dies it could be because it is now daylight and a cloud will come to guide us on if we only look for it.

Reflection: Where might God be leading you today? Is there a situation that, like Egypt, was once a place of safety but you now need to leave? What guides has God sent to help you to travel, by day or by night?

Dear God

You were with Joseph through his trials and tribulations, and in his moments of success. You were with Moses when he faced the Pharaoh and led his people out of Egypt. You were with the people of Israel as they wandered in the wilderness.

I thank You that You are with me now, no matter what I am going through. Give me strength and courage to follow Your guidance, and wisdom to see when the storm is bringing a cloud to lead me to a better place.

Amen

2

Landmarks

"Your word is a lamp for my feet, a light on my path".
(Psalm 119:105)

The sand dunes always
the first familiar sight.
Over the horizon - home.
The lights of Port Elizabeth
twinkling enticingly
across the bay.

Over the years I have travelled this road
time and time again.
Roadside kiosks, anonymous farms,
turnoffs to small towns never seen.

Still my heart lifts
at the sight of the dunes,
sand blowing in the sea breeze.
The city beyond the bay.
Almost home - no longer home.

The landscape of my memory
is written in the sand;
who I was - where I am going.

When I was a child I lived in Port Elizabeth. As a family we travelled a lot, frequently visiting extended family in East London or going on epic caravan expeditions. I didn't have a good sense of place, and because I slept a lot in the car, and I often had no idea where we were. It was only when we reached the Sundays River region that I would recognise the sand dunes and know that we were almost home.

I now know that road well and don't need landmarks to give me direction. I also no longer live in Port Elizabeth so am visiting rather than returning home. But my heart still lifts at the sight of the sand dunes and those memories resurface, of that sleepy child wondering "are we there yet?"

As Christians we know where we are going, but at times the path might seem unclear, or we wonder if we have lost our way. "Are we there yet?' we ask. God gives us guides and landmarks to help us stay on track. These could be verses from the Bible, a sermon, the lyrics of a song, a word of wisdom from a friend or even a memory. Those are the moments that enable us to say "Oh, this is where I am. Now I know where I am".

Reflection: Are there places from your childhood that trigger memories today? Are there landmarks that you look for as you near your home? What markers are in your spiritual life to remind you where you are and where you are going?

 Dear God
Sometimes it feels like I am lost.
Thank You for the landmarks along the way,
the reminders of where I am going
of where I have come from.

At other times it feels
as though I keep going back,
having to deal with the same issues
again and again.

Yet You do not leave me.
You are always with me.
Each time I see a familiar sign
I am reminded of Your love.

Amen

3

The Road Back

*"But one thing I do; forgetting what is behind and straining towards
what is ahead, I press on towards the goal to win the prize for which
God has called me heavenwards in Christ Jesus."*

(Philippians 3:13-14)

It is dusk as we leave PE.
The dying sun
paints the clouds
pastel hues of pink,
casting a glow over
the distant hills.

A last splash of gold
on the river
as we approach Bluewater Bay.
To the right the sea
stretches to the horizon,
columns of fishing rods
stand sentinel,

lines cast into the quiet depths.

The sky fades to grey
as we leave the sunset behind.
The road stretches into the night,
darkness broken by
flashes of distant light.
The cars ahead
leading us home.

As I have mentioned, I grew up in Port Elizabeth (the PE in the poem) but now live in Grahamstown. For some years I was unsure what to answer when asked where I was from. How long do you stay in a town before it becomes home?

I travel between these two towns regularly, frequently returning from a weekend visit on Sunday evenings. When I wrote this poem it was called "The Road Out" and the final line was "leading us back". I was struggling to get it to work. At some point, I remembered that there was another South African poem with that title. When I changed it to "The Road Back" it suddenly all fell into place. It was not, as I had first thought, a poem about leaving Port Elizabeth, but about returning to Grahamstown. This was also when I realised that Grahamstown was, in fact, finally home.

Reflection: Sometimes God calls us into new things, but we resist or are fearful, focused on what we are leaving. We keep looking back at the familiar scenes: the sea, the sunset, the city behind us, reluctant to head into the dark. Yet God is always there, leading us onwards. Leading us home.

Dear God
Thank You for the beauty of this world
and Your constant presence with us in it.
Yet we are reminded that this world
is not our final home.
You have gone ahead
to prepare a place for us
in the Father's house.
Help us to forget what is behind,
to keep our eyes fixed
on the lights ahead
as they lead us home.

Amen

4

Night Drive

"The LORD is my light and my salvation -whom shall I fear? The LORD
is the stronghold of my life – of whom shall I be afraid."
(Psalm 27:1)

A dark night.
A long road
between towns.
No streetlights,
no stars,
barely any other cars.

Our only guides
the cat's eyes
reflecting on the tar
and high above it all,
solitary in the sky,
a Cheshire Cat moon.

When I was a child I was fascinated by cat's eyes, the reflectors used to light up roads. I couldn't figure out how they knew to turn on and off as each car approached. It was only later that I learned they are not lights at all, merely plastic discs reflecting the cars' lights. By daylight they are dull red, barely visible at all.

It can be very dark on the roads between Grahamstown where I live and the nearby cities of Port Elizabeth and East London, to which I travel on a regular basis. For most of the way there are no lights to be seen, and unless it is a weekend there are not many other cars. Looking ahead, there is a small patch of road lit by the headlights, the nearest cat's eye reflecting the headlights, and then utter darkness. If you stopped the car until there was enough light to see ahead, you would wait until morning. Yes, there are lights, leading you on. But they can only be seen as you get close to them.

Sometimes I get frustrated by the darkness in my personal path. I want God to give me a well-lit road so I can see what is coming up ahead. But I need to trust that as I go the cat's eyes will appear, each one lighting up as I approach. If I am not moving there will be nothing to reflect. God lights the way one step at a time.

Reflection: What step is God calling you to take that seems scary? What light has God given you to guide you on your way? Are you reflecting God's light to give other people hope and encouragement?

Dear God

The road is dark. Every time I look ahead I see death, destruction and despair. My small light does not seem strong enough. I keep wanting to wait for more light, more clarity, more courage.

Forgive me for my desire for a fully laid out five-year plan. The uncertainties of this year, with lockdown, disease, death and fear, have shown that our human plans are futile.

Even in this darkness there is light. While the moon is barely visible, I know that it is there. As the days pass the moon will become fuller and brighter. The nights will be less dark. And even if I can't see them now there are cat's eyes on the road ahead, waiting to light up as I get near.

Even in the darkest night I will trust in You. I will step out in faith, taking one step at a time. And I know You will continue to light the path in front of my feet, always guiding me to the next step, the next thing needing to be done.

Thank you that You are the light in my darkness, and You do not leave me alone.

Amen

5

Spring Flowers

"My father's house has many rooms… And if I go and prepare a place
for you, I will come back and take you to be with me that you also may
be where I am. You know the way to the place where I am going."
(John 14:2-4)

"The doctor thinks we shouldn't go.
He's worried about my heart.
I really wanted to see the flowers again,
maybe next year."

Approaching her 90th birthday
my grandmother will not cancel;
sees this as a postponement,
already planning the next trip.

When I first wrote this poem and read it in public someone
commented: "Of course, it is all about death". My response was: "No, it's
about my grandmother going caravanning and her love of the
Namaqualand flowers." Now I can see that it is about both.

My grandparents went caravanning a lot. Many of my childhood holidays were spent travelling with them, a convoy of relations in their different caravans, setting up camp each night and then setting out again the next morning. In their later years, for security, they would go in a group with old friends. Because that took more organising, and, despite their protestations they weren't getting older and slower, they tended to go only once a year. Half the year was spent reminiscing about the last trip and the other half planning the next one. They did not give up the things they loved as they aged, and I suspect this helped to keep them young.

In some ways, this reflects our spiritual journey. We share stories from the past, reading our Bible, listening to the testimonies of others, reflecting on what God has done. But we also look ahead, reading our Bible for guides to the way ahead, listening to God. And while we each travel our own path; we have companions on the journey.

And as we face our mortality, we do not abandon hope. We might leave our bodies, the life we know, but there is another trip ahead to a place where our hearts will be filled with joy. We will see the flowers again.

Reflection: Is there a place you long to visit for the first time or a favourite place you would love to see again? Do you have a "bucket list" of things you want to do or accomplish before you die? What on that list might God be calling you to do?

Dear God

Thank You for the joy of spring, of new life,
the beauty of flowers blooming after a long winter.
As the year passes through its seasons
so our lives follow their seasons.
Help me to look ahead with gladness;
knowing that You are with me
wherever my journey takes me.
Even when I am forced
to slow down, to stay in one place,
I will look ahead,
rest in Your presence,
planning the next trip.

Amen

6
On the Road

"God saw all that he had made and it was very good."

(Genesis 1:31)

Returning from a long holiday
I watch the familiar landscape,
enjoying the recognition
of hills and valleys.

It is dusk; dark clouds
are tinted with the dying light.
Animals appear along
the side of the road.

Apart from the usual horses and cows
I see springbok, kudu, zebra and giraffe.
I keep my eyes peeled,
ever hopeful of finally seeing

one of the lions
whose existence is promised
by the warning signs

and double fences.

We quietly pass the game farms
but my fellow passengers
do not lift their eyes
from their phones.

The small town where I live is 112 miles (180 kilometers) from the nearest city. Most of the road passes through veld, farmland and, increasingly, game farms. It is an hour-and-a-half drive, and I love looking out of the window of the car or bus at the beauty of the natural world. I am always excited to see the wild animals, especially sightings of the elephants or giraffe (I still haven't seen any of the lions). Springbok, zebras and wildebeest are seen so often that they are no more exciting than cows or horses.

It amazes me how many people don't even notice the beauty beside the road, whether it be the animals, the scenery, or the sunsets (which can be stunning). Perhaps because the beauty is always there, it has become routine, barely seen. While there are tourists paying large amounts of money for the experiences, I often experience them during a simple drive between towns.

How often do we do this in other aspects of life? We go along, wrapped up in our thoughts, our concerns, or staring at our phones, and don't look up. We risk missing moments of beauty, signs of God's presence, or areas where our help might be needed.

Reflection: What is distracting you today? Try to set it aside and be aware of what is around you, or what God might be trying to say to you.

 Dear God
Thank you for the beauty of this world.
Open my eyes that I may truly see
What is in front of me.
Forgive me for my distraction,
all the times I don't look properly.
Help me to see this world
with Your eyes
and know that it is good.

Amen

7

Steps of Faith

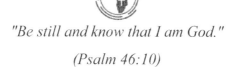

"Be still and know that I am God."

(Psalm 46:10)

I used to live one block
away from my church.
Yet somehow I still struggled
to get there on time;
frequently running up the road
and collapsing into the pew
just before the opening procession.

Now I live further away:
a 15-minute walk there,
20 home, thanks to the hill.
Because I know it takes longer
I don't leave leaving so late
so actually get to church
before the bells stop pealing.

The walk becomes part of the preparation,
a time to think and to pray,
to sing songs in my head,

to praise God for the beauty around me.
The return walk a chance to reflect
on the service, the sermon;
to really hear what God is saying.

I used to think that being super close to my church was a good thing, and it was. But in some ways, it made it too easy to just rush into services, my mind still filled with the daily "stuff" of my life. And because it only took three minutes to get there, I constantly underestimated how much time I actually had and always seemed to leave too late and then have to rush.

Sometimes a bit of distance can help, as I found when I moved a few years ago. Because it now takes me longer to get to church, I have more time to calm my mind and focus on God. Even if I am sleepy or distracted, the quietness of Sunday mornings in a small town, the beauty of the trees I walk past, the distant hills, the skies and clouds, lift my spirit. And as I walk, the tall spire of the church rises above the town, like a lighthouse guiding me home.

During the long months of lockdown, I have attended church in my lounge, logged onto Facebook for a live video service. I am grateful for the technology that allows this, and for all the work done to keep us connected. But it is easy to be distracted, to log in at the last minute or to stay online and start doing other things straight away. I have learned to give myself 15 minutes before the service (the time it took me to walk to church) listening to worship music to calm my mind. As I sit at my computer, I look out the window and see the church spire, an antenna helping to focus my thoughts.

Reflection: It can be too easy to get caught up in busyness, racing from one thing to another. For me, a walk was a good way to set aside space for prayer and reflection. And now in lockdown, listening to music helps me to settle down before church. What can you do to ensure that you have quiet spaces to focus on God?

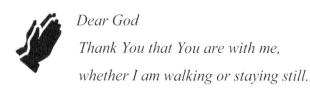

Dear God
Thank You that You are with me,
whether I am walking or staying still.
Forgive me for the times
when I have been so busy
rushing around
that I have missed
Your presence.
Help me to hear Your word
despite the busyness of my life,
and to make spaces
for quiet and reflection.

Amen

About the Author

Crystal Warren was born and raised in Port Elizabeth but has lived in Makhanda (formerly Grahamstown) for the last 30 years. She has studied librarianship, history and English literature, and has worked as a librarian, literary researcher and museum curator. Her poems and stories have been published in many literary journals and anthologies. She has two poetry collections, *Bodies of Glass* and *Predictive Text* and one children's story *What's in the Pot?* published. She is poet in residence at the Cathedral of St George and St Michael in Makhanda.

Other Books by Crystal Warren

Bodies of Glass. Poems published by Aerial Publishing (Grahamstown), 2004

Predictive Press. Poems published by Modjaji Press (Cape Town), 2019
Order in print from publisher
E-book available from Amazon

What's in the Pot? Children's book with illustrations and design by Hayley Alonzo and Rat Western published online by Book Dash (Cape Town), 2018, and in print 2020

Sunrise to Sunset

"7 Landscapes of Africa"

CHRISTIAN DEVOTIONAL

DERYN VAN DER TANG

SUNRISE TO SUNSET

Acknowledgements

I would like to thank Hannah Marie MacIntosh and Robert Read for their thoughtful suggestions, insight and editing.

A special thanks to Phillip Read for making the travel to Namibia and Victoria Falls possible and for the rest of the family for their encouragement along the way.

I would also like to thank Louise Morse and Justina Ford for their mentorship in my writing journey and CWOSA for their support and giving me this opportunity.

Table of Contents

Introduction

The places I have been and lived in Africa will always be a part of me. Hence my theme, "Landscapes." I was born in Rhodesia (Zimbabwe) and was entranced with the sunsets over the Zambezi River. The glory of African sunrises and sunsets cannot be beaten. I have memories of many a dawn call to go game viewing as well, but dawn in the Namibian desert was the most spiritual I have experienced. I wanted to share it with you, my readers.

The other themes of the sprightly springbok, climbing a mountain, the eagle and crossing the river, are all things that have been meaningful to me as I pursue my relationship with God, and I see how He can communicate with us through His creation. It was my joy to introduce my eldest son's new Finnish family to my land of birth.

1
Sunrise Over Namibia

"Very early on Sunday morning, just at sunrise, they went to the tomb."
(Mark 16:2)
"His coming is as brilliant as the sunrise. Rays of light flash from his
hands, where his awesome power is hidden."
(Habakkuk 3:4)

It was our first trip to Namibia to show my new Finnish family Africa, the land of my birth. We had travelled to the Namib Naukluft Lodge as a base so we could see the desert. Our wakeup call was at 4:45am to have a mini breakfast before we set out for the Sossusvlei sand dunes.

The moon and stars were spectacular as we travelled in the dark. The magnificence of the night skies made us aware of how infinite the Universe is. The stars sparkled and twinkled in the thick velvet blackness, and the indigo silhouette of the distant mountains framed the bottom edge of this picture. The sickle moon and the morning star were set in place between the ridge of the mountains and the expanse of the skies above. It was a moment of timelessness, when we felt part of the picture and not detached from it.

Towards 6.00am, the first light of dawn started to show behind the ridge of mountains in the east, and the velvet blackness of the night sky slowly turned into pale blue. Fingers of sunlight faded the stars from sight. The sickle moon and morning star hung there a little longer before they took their closing bow when the curtain of daylight was finally lifted.

Moses and Aaron were the guardians of the Tabernacle in the wilderness and were told to camp on the east side towards the sunrise. Dawn is the time when your body, mind and soul are rested, and you can spend quiet time meditating, praying and worshiping God before other activities demand your attention. It is a time to wait on the Lord for instructions for the day ahead, to be thankful for new opportunities and a time to sit and be part of the greater picture of things. Your individual importance disappears as it is absorbed into the ebb and flow of the common experience of those around us.

The soft blush of daybreak brightens as the sun rises higher in the sky; the shadows are softer at first light. I like to think that dawn is the space for new beginnings, new thoughts, new attitudes, new deeds, a time for new perspectives before they become hardened dogmas and points of view. Sunrise gives me space to think of the greater good, that I am merely one mortal among thousands. We all take our place in the overall welfare of mankind by the actions that come from our waking up and starting each day right. Let the softness of love be our shadows and not the sharp edges drawn by the noonday sun.

It was dawn when Mary found the empty tomb. Jesus, also called the *bright and morning star,* conquered the final enemy, death. Seeing the morning star shine so brightly in the desert reminded me of the importance of dawn and our starting the day right.

- How important is it that we honor the first few hours of each new day in spiritual practice?

- In what way can you see this make a difference to your day?

- What part can you play today in the greater good?

 Dear God, thank you that I can wake up to a new day. Your mercies are sufficient to cover what this day has in store for me.

2

Your Destiny is in the Desert

"He changes rivers into deserts, and springs of water into dry, thirsty
land."
(Psalm 107:35)
"Restore our fortunes, Lord, as streams renew the desert."
(Isaiah 35:1)

The rocky outcrops gradually turned into sand dunes and the
vegetation became very sparse in the arid conditions of the Namib
Desert. We saw ostrich and springbok as they searched for food amongst
rock and dry scrub along the way. We drove to the entrance of the
Sossusvlei National Park, where we transferred into 4 x 4 vehicles
equipped for driving in the dry sandy riverbed which served as a road.
The vehicle slithered and bucked along this track until we arrived at the
Kameeldoring picnic spot. Here the driver unpacked a picnic breakfast
which was most welcome. A flock of sparrows jostled and tweeted
waiting for crumbs. They obviously knew the breakfast drill! One brave
sparrow jumped onto my shoe and tried to snatch food from my hand.

The undulating dunes were on every side of us with their high, sharp curved ridges and hollowed wind-carved sides. The great purple shadows and patterns thrown by the sunlight make these dunes a photographer's paradise. We set off to climb Dune 17, Big Mamma. We walked along the ridge. It was not too difficult walking, but progress was slow. Near the top I decided to stop and just "be" so I could have a time of quiet. Walking with the group was a distraction from my desert experience.

To me, a desert experience needed to be a time of total silence and solitude when I could just listen to God's voice with no distraction. I sat with my fingers sifting through the sand of the dune. I listened to the silence; it was palpable. Not a sound, not a cry of a bird or even the sound of voices as the tour group disappeared over the ridge. It was a moment of being at one with the sand, one with the space around me, isolated in the middle of the vast acres of sand, yet quite at peace as I let the silence fill me. I watched an ant run down the side of the dune and a desert lizard make its way across the sand.

I wondered how creatures could live in such a harsh environment. Although the desert appeared to be dead, it was still very much alive. The longer I sat there the more I realized I was not alone!

I thought of Moses and the burning bush, Jesus' temptation in the wilderness, and all those desert fathers who went into the wilderness to find 'something'. There is a saying 'your destiny is determined in the desert.' It is during those times of dryness and apparent lifelessness that thoughts and temptations to give up make their presence felt. It is during the dry times in our life, the times when we do not have the energy or the inclination to move forward, when we feel empty, that we thirst for something bigger than ourselves to take over.

Once you have experienced the overwhelming desolation of the desert, you will never be the same. When the deep place of silence filters into the very core of your being, that is where you meet with God and return, ready to continue with your mission in life. There is a paradox in this experience; before we can flow with renewed energy, we need this time of dryness to push our roots deeper into God.

As I sat there on the ridge, the silence became a song, I could just feel the praise and worship welling up like a spring of inner joy. Prayer flowed naturally as a conversation with God. I prayed for rain as it was so dry, and I prayed for hope for the future. When I felt full and complete after being in this holy place, I set off down the dune again to join the rest of the group at the vehicle and we drove back to the Namib Naukluft Lodge. This desert experience was one I will never forget, enabling me to experience a heightened encounter of God's presence.

▪When do you feel the need for solitude and renewal?

▪After a period of dryness in your life, did you bloom again with renewed vision and energy?

 Thank you God for the times of dryness when our soul thirsts for something bigger than ourselves. You refresh us from within, with your Living Water.

3

As Surefooted as the Springbok

*"As the deer longs for streams of water, so I long for you, O God. I thirst
for God, the living God. When can I go and stand before him?"*
(Psalm 42:1-2)
*"Her princes are like starving deer searching for pasture. They are too
weak to run from the pursuing enemy"*
(Lamentations 1:6)

During our drive through Namibia, we were privileged to see several
groups of springbok grazing in the arid veld as they searched for the odd
blade of grass or root. These fascinating deer with their characteristic
white faces, black stripes, tan triangle on their forehead, and curved
horns are probably South Africa's most iconic animal. When alarmed,
they have an unusual way of jumping. They 'pronk' extremely high with
stiff legs while they run, which is quite unique to them. Living in the dry
and arid regions of Southern Africa, they have adapted well to their
rocky surroundings, feeding off scrub and some grasses. They have a
preference for plants that have a higher water content such as roots or
flowers when in season. Their large herds migrate across great distances
searching for food and water.

For me, the springbok represents one of the Biblical metaphors of surefootedness and thirsting after God. These beautiful creatures make an amazing sight when they 'pronk'. They can jump vertically up to three-and-a-half meters high and then land perfectly on all four hooves before 'pronking' off again. The Old Testament mentions on numerous occasions that "He makes me as surefooted as a deer, enabling me to stand on mountain heights." Deer are God's messengers of stability when we are navigating difficult territory. When we are alarmed, afraid, or running from danger, we can head for the higher ground knowing that we will still be able to stand. We will overcome, even though fighting the enemy is on difficult terrain. The Lord will guide our footsteps and we can stand securely in the knowledge that His presence is with us at all times.

Yet there are times when we just cannot seem to connect with God. We yearn for His comfort and presence. It is in those times of spiritual drought that, like the springbok, we travel through the desolate places searching for refreshment. Our hearts long for God and we lament that we are like starving deer searching for pasture, too weak to fight off the enemy. There are times we feel too vulnerable to carry on when God is nowhere to be found. We feel we are about to fall into the hands of the enemy because our resistance has weakened. We long for God to rescue us. The springbok knows a predator will catch them in their weakened state if they do not continue to search for the stream or waterhole or dig until they find a root to give them sustenance. Sometimes we too have to dig a very deep well to find that spring of water in the desert, or spend time searching the Scriptures for that root that will take us to the promise of God's help and presence in times of need.

- Where do you run to when you are afraid?

- Are you satisfied with the small 'nibbles' or are you looking for the flowing stream or waterhole?

 God, sometimes it is hard to find you when we search for you and long for you to rescue us from our enemies. Lead us to the water, sustain us with your words, let us find our stability in your Presence.

4
Reaching the Summit

"A song for pilgrims ascending to Jerusalem. I look up to the mountains— does my help come from there?"
(Isaiah 49:13)
"I press on towards the goal to win the prize for which God has called me heavenwards in Christ Jesus. All of us who are mature should take such a view of things. And if on some point you think differently that too God will make clear to you. Only let us live up to what we have already attained".
(Phil 3:14-16)

I had been living in Cape Town for several years and enjoyed the beautiful walks and hikes around Table Mountain. One of my goals was to see the wildflowers in the Overberg, but for various reasons I had not been able join a hiking group to do it. I planned a weekend away with my other son to visit the area and do the ten-kilometer hike through the Caledon Wildflower Garden and environs. We stayed at the Caledon Hotel, so we could enjoy the hot spring water in the Victorian Bath House as well.

We were well prepared with adequate clothing, shoes and refreshments, and we set off with a map to guide us. We anticipated a pleasant and leisurely walk through the beautiful countryside at wildflower time. We found the trail and started to walk; enjoying the scenery, the fresh air, and the fact we were at last on our way to fulfill my dream.

We stopped occasionally to enjoy the flowers and the view. Winding its way out of the gardens at the far end, the path became narrower and a bit steeper and it took more effort to walk. We slowed our pace a bit, but I got tired. My legs ached, and blood pounded through my temples as the pathway wound its way upwards. We met unexpected difficulties crossing a vlei and small stream and our shoes got wet. We had to stop frequently for me to take a breather and a sip of water.

The path continued to wind steeply upwards, unrelenting as we headed for the top of the mountain (which was not shown on the map!). We persevered. My goal was to complete this hike. My son patiently waited for me so I could rest often, and encouraged me along the way. As we approached the summit, the way became very rough and stony. The pathway almost disappeared. In places, I had to crawl on all fours to make my way upward. How I wished there was an easier way, but I had to persevere. There was no turning back. We were closer to the top than the gardens at the bottom. To go back would have been just as difficult as well as an admission of defeat of my dream. I chose to keep moving forward with every step, no matter how difficult it was and however tired I felt.

Eventually, we reached the summit and saw the world stretched out below us. It was breathtaking in every direction, despite the freezing wind. We had a whole new perspective and could see the path we had travelled in the distance, far below. We pointed to obstacles we had overcome. They looked so small from up there. We sheltered behind a rock and rested awhile before it was time to climb back down. The descent was just as difficult. The path was unclear. The way was strewn with boulders, stones, and loose gravel. We slipped and stumbled our way down. We did not require as much rest although it was just as difficult, but eventually we arrived back at the car having attained our goal and fulfilled my dream.

After this experience, I reflected on my Christian walk. I wondered, do I expect everything to be easy without obstacles and difficulties, traversing life's pathways? No. Difficulties will always be there, trials of our faith and character are part of our growth to become more Christlike. Just as my son was there to encourage me, Jesus has promised to be with us and never leave nor forsake us. When we have started out and difficulties arise, do we doubt we are on the right road? Not if we are sure we're going the way the Lord has directed us. The goal is still there. The way may not be clear, but the goal does not change. Our human frailty does get in the way and we may have to stop to take a breath to be refreshed but we do not give up. Lack of resources may slow the process down, but that does not change our goal or mission.

I once saw an old priest on his bicycle in the middle of the tsetse-fly-ridden Zambezi Valley in Zimbabwe. He was hundreds of kilometers from anywhere, going to serve his people. How many of us would be prepared to go to that length to serve?

We can become enthusiastic with the vision and set a good goal for ourselves. This is the exciting part, the beginning of the journey, just as I had eagerly planned the trip to Caledon to visit the Wildflower Gardens. Once we are physically involved in reaching that goal, difficulties and problems become apparent. We may feel like giving up. Self-doubt sets in and we wonder if we are really on the right path. Did we fully understand our calling? Or have we perhaps taken a wrong turn somewhere and we are headed in the wrong direction? Our enthusiasm wanes, we are discouraged and the motivation to attain the goal diminishes.

We need to persevere and not grow weary but know that the Lord is with us. Our map is His Word which is a guide and a lamp for our feet. He knows the obstacles we face. They are there as learning tools. We are encouraged by His Word and our fellow travelers along the way, and we can rest in Him from time to time.

Yes, the upward slog is hard, but when you reach the summit or attain your goal, the hard work will be worth it. You will see what has been accomplished from a higher perspective. Keep going!

▪In what times in your life do you feel it is just too hard to keep going?

▪Who can you ask, or what can you do, for some encouragement to continue the journey?

Lord, we look to you when the going gets tough, sometimes we think we are just not going to make it. Help us to persevere.

Your Presence is always there to encourage us and your Word there to guide us.

193

5

Soaring Like an Eagle

"Even youths will become weak and tired, and young men will fall in exhaustion. But those who trust in the Lord will find new strength. They will soar high on wings like eagles. They will run and not grow weary. They will walk and not faint."
(Isaiah 40:30-31)
"He fills my life with good things. My youth is renewed like the eagle's! The Lord gives righteousness and justice to all who are treated unfairly."
(Psalm 106:5,6)

As we stood at the top of the Overberg mountain and looked as far as the eye could see, my son pointed out two eagles as they circled high on the thermals. We were amazed to think that the eagles could see prey far below, where we could only make out the larger objects. Small things merged into a colored blur. Eagles can have a wingspan of up to two meters across, they soar to great heights and look graceful and effortless as they let the thermal currents carry them. They have clear vision and patience to wait for the appropriate moment to strike, then, from a great height they swoop down in seconds onto their prey.

The eagle has significant symbolism in mythology, human culture, and in Christianity. As an artist, I love the spiritual metaphors of the

Bible. What is it about the eagle that lends itself to the mystery and symbolism of God's Word?

Initially, God spoke through nature and through creation, so that man would have no excuse for not seeing Him as the Creator God. In the Church of England, it is tradition to place the Bible on the outstretched wings of a bronze eagle.

When an eagle catches a snake, it does not fight it on the ground. It picks it up and flies up with it, then drops it back to the ground. A snake has no stamina, power or balance in the air. It is useless, weak and vulnerable, whereas on the ground it is deadly, wise and powerful. The eagle teaches us to take our battles to the spiritual realm as it lifts its lethal and toxic prey away from where it can do damage. When you take problems that can harm you to the spiritual realm and pray for deliverance from evil, God takes charge. Don't fight these battles in the physical realm—move to a higher realm, like an eagle. You will be assured of a clear victory.

I see this symbol as the power of the Holy Spirit rising above the earth, a freedom rising above the material to see spiritual things, power, balance, dignity and grace, attaining a higher truth, the messenger between heaven and earth. We should be waiting for that moment of Divine truth when the Holy Spirit is ready to use us and work through us.

The metaphor of the eagle teaches us that we can trust in the Lord with patient expectation. He will fulfill the promises in His Word to strengthen us to rise above life's difficulties. He will protect us from evil. God loves us and wants the best for us, so we can relax and be confident that His purposes are right. We need to be fully convinced that He has the power to control all of life as well as ours. Though our faith may be weak or struggling, we can accept His provision, protection, and care for us.

We are encouraged by Isaiah's words that even young people will get tired and give up. But if we wait on the Lord, He will give us renewed energy and strength for the battle. The Psalmist also used the eagle as a symbol of renewed energy as he was praising God for His help against injustice.

Sometimes we may feel insignificant and helpless as we struggle against unjust systems. When we get weary it is good to remember the battle is not ours. The war is against the principalities and powers of darkness. When we take our issues up into the spiritual realm, our Lord will fight them with His heavenly army.

After our refreshing break at the top of the Overberg mountain, my son and I took one last look at the eagles as they effortlessly soared and circled above us. We made our way down the mountain back into the physical realm of practical daily living. We had learnt a valuable spiritual lesson from the eagles. Anxiety ends where faith begins, when we take our battles off the ground to a higher plane.

•What Battles are you facing that need to be taken off the physical to the spiritual realm?

•Do you believe that God's justice will prevail in the end?

Father, sometimes I feel so weary of life's battles. I see injustice and unfairness all around me. It impacts my life, my family and community's life. There seems no ending to the struggles. Please may I just hand them to you?

6

Crossing the River

"When you go through deep waters, I will be with you. When you go through rivers of difficulty, you will not drown. When you walk through the fire of oppression, you will not be burned up; the flames will not consume you."
(Isaiah 43:2)

"And I will fix your boundaries from the Red Sea to the Mediterranean Sea, and from the eastern wilderness to the Euphrates River."
(Exodus 23:31)

"But you will soon cross the Jordan River and live in the land the Lord your God is giving you. When he gives you rest from all your enemies and you're living safely in the land, you must bring everything I command you."
(Deuteronomy 12:10)

No visit to showcase Africa to our Finnish family would have been complete without a visit to one of my favorite places, the Victoria Falls and the mighty Zambezi River. When you walk through the forest when the river is full, you get soaked to the skin with spray whether you wear rain clothes or not. The local name for the Falls is 'Mosi-oa-Tunya, "The Smoke that Thunders," because the noise of the water is so loud you cannot hear yourself speak. David Livingstone was the first European to discover these falls. His statue stands near to the Devil's Cataract where a rainbow forms over the falling water.

The Victoria Falls is a great tourist attraction and World Heritage site, where a lot of adventure sports like white water rafting and bungee jumping can be experienced. The Zambezi River serves as the northern boundary between Zimbabwe and Zambia. The far northwestern tip of Zimbabwe is where the Caprivi Strip, Botswana, and Zambia all meet at the Zambezi river which serves as boundary to all four states.

This ancient river starts in the upper reaches of Zambia near the Congo border. After the Victoria Falls, it flows through Lake Kariba and the Cahora Bassa Hydro Electric scheme which provides electricity and water management for the region. It finally makes its way through Mozambique into the Indian Ocean.

We took a helicopter trip above the waterfall and along the river. The sinuous ribbon of water lay far below us, dotted with islands. We saw it rush its way to the gorge where it fell in thundering chaos over the precipice to the bottom of the ancient chasm carved out over eons and then on to its destination.

The southern border of Zimbabwe is demarcated by the 'great, grey, greasy Limpopo River' as Rudyard Kipling described it. Rivers form natural boundaries for countries and wars have been fought to hold their ground, often being the place where the battle was lost or won.

God said he would fix the boundaries of the Promised Land from the Red Sea to the Mediterranean Sea, and from the eastern wilderness to the

Euphrates River. Crossing the Jordan has become a metaphor for transitions. When the Israelites entered the Promised Land, the Jordan parted. They went across to start a new life in the land of milk and honey.

The River Jordan again parted when Elijah crossed and ascended to heaven after giving his mantle to Elisha, transitioning him into his new prophetic role. Another personal transition took place when Naaman dipped in the river and his leprosy was healed. After wrestling with God at the River Jabbok, Jacob was named Israel, as he transitioned to become the father of the Israelites.

Crossing the Jordan can also be a metaphor for transitioning from spiritual darkness into spiritual awakening. John the Baptist baptized Jesus in the River Jordan, transitioning the New Covenant when the heavens opened to announce that this was God's Son and from this time our centuries would now be counted from AD instead of BC.

When I crossed the Limpopo River into South Africa, I left one country and culture and transitioned into another. There was also the national transition in November 1965 when our country, which was known as Rhodesia, changed from being a self-governing British territory to an independent sovereign state which would eventually be known as Zimbabwe.

There are also personal transitions, from being married to being widowed. One day, we will all face our final 'crossing the Jordan,' a euphemistic term for death. Christ's atoning death on the cross and resurrection assures us that those who believe in Him, when we exit this life, will transition into our new heavenly life. "Crossing the river" is a timeless metaphor for death in mythology and different cultures where various rituals are practiced to help the person into the afterlife.

As we completed our visit to the Victoria Falls and the Zambezi, I realized how difficult transitions can be. We had to adjust to our new state of being part of the Finnish family, just as they had to adjust to being part of our African family. We can be encouraged by the Word of God. Jesus says He will be with us as we go through these difficult times and adapt to our new circumstances. We also learn to set boundaries that keep us safe and preserve our authentic selves so that the transition does not change who we are, but enriches us.

•What transitions have you made where you had to metaphorically 'cross the river'?

•What are your thoughts and fears around the final 'crossing the Jordon?'

•What boundaries do you need to set?

Father God, there are times that I am overwhelmed, and I need to hold my ground and set boundaries. There are times when you have set my boundaries and I must trust that you will be with me and I will not be overcome.

7

Sunset Over the Zambezi

"And don't sin by letting anger control you. Don't let the sun go down while you are still angry."

(Ephesians 4:26)

"There was a man named Nicodemus, a Jewish religious leader who was a Pharisee. After dark one evening, he came to speak with Jesus. "Rabbi," he said, "we all know that God has sent you to teach us. Your miraculous signs are evidence that God is with you."

(John 3:1)

The ultimate experience of Africa to me is sunset. I have yet to encounter something more glorious than a sunset cruise down the Zambezi River above the Victoria Falls.

We arrived at the river boat at late afternoon and set sail up the mighty Zambezi. We settled back to enjoy a glass of wine and snacks. The boat quietly chugged up the river alongside the banks and islands as we looked at birds and wildlife. We were rewarded by seeing a variety of birds, as well as hippopotami that bobbed up and down in the water, opening their great yawning mouths. We could hear the evening chirping of the birds as they circled, argued, and settled in the branches of trees for the night. We listened to the call of some animals and were fortunate enough to see a number of warthogs as they dipped to drink at the water's edge. We passed a stately kudu bull with his spiral horns, strolling along the riverbank, also come to get his evening drink.

After a pleasant couple of hours cruising up the Zambezi River we watched the sun start to slowly sink down the horizon. The water gently lapped against the sides of the boat. The green landscape morphed into deep purple shadows. Palm trees stood out as silhouettes against the glowing sky. The path of the sun across the water turned the river into molten gold. I have only ever seen such an exquisite sunset on the Zambezi. We sat in awe appreciating every glowing color of God's palette, a glorious ending to the day. Near the equator, the sun sinks quite quickly, and it was soon below the horizon and it was time to head back to the hotel. We left the boat with a sense of having met with God in the peace and awe of His Creation.

In the Jewish culture, sunset signifies the end of the day. The outcasts, sick, and demon-possessed came to Jesus secretly after dark to be healed. These people were afraid of what others may say or think. A Jewish leader in law and religion, Nicodemus, came to Jesus after dark when he wanted to find out more and have his questions answered.

Sunset is the time of day when we are told to put our worries aside and any anger and problems behind us. If we have experienced a difficult day and hold grudges or anger against someone, Scripture warns us not to let the sun set on our anger. If we have questions to ask, we can lay them down now. There is a good reason for this emotionally and spiritually. When we bring all the troubles of the day to God and ask for forgiveness from those whom we have upset during the day or who have upset us, our minds are stilled. Our hearts can be ready and open to receive answers and love from God again as we worship Him. A clear conscience and mind will let us have untroubled sleep. In the morning, we will be in the right frame of mind to let love flow back into our lives and find solutions to our problems.

The setting sun on the Zambezi was a glowing reminder to me that I should always honor God.

- Are you looking for answers to questions that you are afraid to ask publicly?

- Is there anyone you need to forgive?

- What would it feel like to close your day with a clear conscience and an open heart?

 Father, I lay down the burdens of this day at your feet, let me forgive those who have hurt me, bless my family and friends, let your love enfold us all that we may be at peace for the night.

About the Author

Deryn is a writer, artist, and lover of nature and travel. Born in the previously named Rhodesia (now Zimbabwe) from 1820 Settler pioneering stock, she has travelled the world, moving to South Africa and the United Kingdom. She retired from her career of an exploration cartographer and housing manager and now lives in the United States of America. Her rich adventures have enabled her to write about transforming life's experiences.

Deryn is a contributing author/illustrator to several books and has had travel articles published in the Senior Travel Expert and contributed to PFS in-house magazine. She writes for her two blogs "Under The Msasa Tree" which covers travel and family stories, and "Crossing My Bridges" which is about transitions through grief, new destinations, and the second half of life. She has also contributed to "How 7 Women of Faith Manifest GODLY Success Through Spiritual Intimacy," an Amazon Bestseller in the Christian Liberation Section.

NOTE FROM THE AUTHOR: *If you enjoyed these meditative reflections on African Landscapes and would like to read my blogs and get a Newsletter from time to time, please sign up for my mailing list on "Crossing My Bridges".*

Seven lights
for dark times

Dianne J. Wilson

SEVEN LIGHTS FOR DARK TIMES

Penned in South Africa, edited in America and aimed at an international, multi-cultural audience, 7 Lights for Dark Times may have a conglomeration of South African and USA spelling, and phraseology. I hope you read through all that and get the heart behind the words.

Table of Contents

Dear Reader

Before you start reading this devotional, I want one fact to settle into you so deeply that it engraves itself into your DNA.

You are deeply, irrevocably, loved by the God of the Universe.

There is nothing you can do (or not do) that is going to change His mind about you.

He knows, and understands, everything about you and He loves you anyway.

If you need proof of this, go read John 3:16 and insert your name where it says 'the world'.

Our world is broken and we deal with the consequences of this daily. I'm writing from Africa, but if there's one thing 2020 has taught us, it's that no place on earth is immune to suffering.

My hope in writing this devotional booklet is to offer a different perspective on hard times, difficult circumstances, and situations that don't seem to line up with the heart of a loving Heavenly Father.

With love,

Di

My Gift To You

Receive your free copy of *Messy Life—Chasing Your Passions Through the Chaos of Normal Life* when you sign up at www.diannejwilson.com.

You'll also be first in the queue for any book news and specials.

1

Broken, But Not Disqualified

"But he said to me, 'My grace is sufficient for you, for my power is made perfect in weakness.' Therefore I will boast all the more gladly about my weaknesses, so that Christ's power may rest on me."
(2 Corinthians 12:9)

My smoothie maker broke. To understand the magnitude of those four little words, here's the context … I'm not a big breakfast eater, but I do know that our bodies need fuel to do what we need them to. Getting a smoothie maker changed my life. I toss a whole bunch of good things in there, whizz it up, chug it down, and I'm set for the day.

Until it broke.

It started as a hairline crack in the base that holds the blade on the jug and keeps the liquid in. Each time I used it, that crack grew until it finally snapped altogether. The rest of the bits were all fine, but that bottom part kind of held it all together. It was an early morning, with a full day to get through and no smoothie in sight. I panicked.

I tried wrapping elastic around it, but it rolled up the moment I put the jug into the base. I had the same problem with tape and anything else I tried. In desperation, I closed my eyes, shoved the broken thing into the base, and made a smoothie. I held my breath, towel in hand to mop up the mess.

It worked. There was no splatter, no leaking, no disastrous mess. What?!

I've been using it broken for weeks now, and we're still going strong. It turns out that the most important part holding it all together is the base.

Do you ever do that? Look at your brokenness and decide that you're disqualified? You're just too wrecked to be useful to God or anyone else. Jesus could never use you to make a difference in somebody's life because yours isn't perfect.

It's easy to think that, but it's not how He works.

I know, I've lived there. It's a horrible place to be. You want your life to matter, but each time you think about stepping up, you're confronted with your own short-comings and you back down.

Here's the thing, you and I will never be completely whole this side of Heaven, but God is the base that holds you together and makes it possible for you to function despite your brokenness.

He delights in working with us on His projects as we are. You may find yourself thinking … but if He knew, He wouldn't trust me with that. Well, friend, He knows and it's *Him in you* and *you in Him* that will get the job done.

There are things that God has hand-picked for you to do for Him. He chose you, fully aware of all the things that you think would disqualify you. In Him, those things don't matter. He wants you to do it anyway.

~ Thought for the Day ~

Can you list the things that have stopped you doing what you feel God has called you to do?

Are you ready to surrender that list to Him and get busy with His work for you?

 Dear Lord, help me let go of the idea that I have to be perfect before You can use me. Give me a clear understanding of what our next project together is.

2

Light vs Dark—It's A Kingdom Thing

"You are all children of the light and children of the day. We do not belong to the night or to the darkness."

(1 Thessalonians 5:5)

When I was a little girl, I tried hard to be someone that God would like. I would do my best not to do a single thing that would upset Him. You see, I wanted to live in the light and the only way to do that—in my mind—was to be perfect, to have no darkness in me.

I remember reciting *The Lord's Prayer* after lights-out in my bed at night. I didn't really know what the words meant, but I waved it at Heaven as some sort of peace offering. I longed to be acceptable, and accepted.

Yet, no matter how hard I tried, I could never make it past a few hours without yelling at the dog, or taking an extra cookie without asking, or doing any one of a million petty things that I thought disqualified me.

(I also tried to get skinny when I was a teenager by only eating lettuce. That lasted half-an-hour and was about as successful as the whole *never being naughty* thing.)

Each time I failed, I felt as if the darkness inside me was winning. Growing. Taking over. I ended up feeling hopeless. I could never live up to God's standards and because of that, I would never be acceptable enough to Him that He would let me get close.

I came to the conclusion that I just wasn't good enough to live in the light. Knowing Him personally was never going to be an option for me because I couldn't get my act together, no matter how hard I tried.

But then I heard the story of two kingdoms.

One kingdom was ruled by a cruel despot. He demanded absolute loyalty and required soul-shredding sacrifices of those in his kingdom. In return? Nothing. He didn't care about his subjects, he didn't look after them or provide for them. Yet the citizens stayed out of fear and some twisted sense of loyalty and belonging.

The other kingdom was under the rule of a king who loved his subjects. He treated them fairly and made sure their needs were met. He protected them from their enemies and fought to keep them safe. In his kingdom, there was no lack, no poverty, and no hunger. He loved his subjects and they loved him.

So here's the thing, being a child of the light and not the darkness is not about successfully skipping through a minefield of do's and don'ts.

It is all about which King you choose to belong to. Think of it this way: When we moved from Boksburg to East London, we became East Londoners. As we relocated, our identity changed.

It's the same with your spiritual identity. As you choose which kingdom to step into, you choose what will rule over you—darkness or light.

That simple choice, right there, is far more important than any other decision you will make in your life. It's not about what you do or don't do, but about who you choose.

As you step into His kingdom, you step into His care, His provision, His love, and open access to Him 24/7.

~ Thought for the Day ~

Have you stepped into the Kingdom of Light—God's Kingdom?

What do you need from your King today?

 Dear Lord, thank You that I can step into Your Kingdom. Thank You that as I do that, I will have access to all your goodness and provision.

3

Not Meant For You

(A perspective on hardship and disappointment)

"Praise be to the God and Father of our Lord Jesus Christ, the Father of compassion and the God of all comfort, who comforts us in all our troubles, so that we can comfort those in any trouble with the comfort we ourselves receive from God."

(2 Corinthians 1:3-4)

My youngest daughter was diagnosed with scoliosis. She'd been doing gymnastics for a few months, was showing promise, and had been chosen to compete for the first time. Her every spare second was spent upside down as she worked on handstands and walk-overs. It all unraveled with a few x-rays, a diagnosis, and a truckload of fear.

As her mom, I felt helpless. She cried. She was a physically active young lady who also danced. All she wanted was to be "normal," work on her strength, and do things without fear of injury. She didn't want her friends to know, as though having a skewed spine was somehow shameful. My heart was so sore for her and I couldn't help asking, "God, what are You doing?"

It took me a long time to get over the disappointment of God going off my script. (Really, God? What were You thinking?) It's one thing to work through disappointment as an adult, but for a parent to watch your child struggle through something? Not fun at all.

Yet the more I prayed, the more peace I felt that He was taking her on a journey to establish things in her character that wouldn't have been there otherwise. My child has always had her heart set on being a doctor. Doctors have to face patients and deliver verdicts of life-changing news and can help their patients see hope in the future, regardless. Could she honestly do that if her life had been nothing but sunshine and roses? I began to see the connection.

In His infinite wisdom, He risked breaking our trust to allow something that would shape her in ways He could use. Now? She's exercising under careful supervision to balance out the imbalances in her muscles. She's still dancing and has gone from not wanting anyone to know, to being able to speak about it openly.

Jesus is walking this journey with her, holding her every step of the way and I'm floored by the growth in my kid.

As a believer, I've subconsciously assumed that I should have some sort of immunity against hardships or disappointment. Does this mean I believe that God "sends" sickness or hurt into our lives as lessons? Absolutely not. I do believe that He is able to use every awkward, horrible, painful thing that this broken world might bat our way. He promised that much to us in His Word.

Nothing is wasted, He can use it all. When He gets involved, there is always beauty in the outcome of our trials and sufferings–even if we don't get to see it in this world.

Dear friend, maybe some of the things that come your way are not intended for you at all, but are to make you more useful to others who are suffering. That's quite a thought.

~ Thought for the Day ~

What have you experienced that has been hard for you to make peace with?

Have you been able to use what you learned through your experience to help someone else?

 Dear Lord, help me understand that no pain is wasted when I trust You with my life. I ask You to help me recognize those that you send my way.

4

A Hunter's Focus

"Now to him who is able to do immeasurably more than all we ask or imagine, according to his power that is at work within us..." (Ephesians 3:20)

In the days before supermarkets, when a man was hungry, he would either have to go hunting, or go digging around for some fruit, tubers, or nuts. If he were more inclined to get his protein from meat, he'd have to find a suitable buck, track it for hours, and patiently wait until the right moment to let his arrows or bullets fly.

If he were more vegetarian in nature, he'd swap a bow and gun for a shovel, aim himself at the veggie patch, and spend a few hours digging and harvesting. Either way, his focused efforts would be rewarded with a full tummy.

So, imagine with me for a moment: What do you think would happen if he were to sit and stare at his hungry belly all day?

He'd likely starve to death while his belly rumbled.

A hunter, or gatherer, is completely focused on his prey or his crops, or, put in other words—the answer to his problem.

When a problem comes my way, my natural inclination is to focus on it. I pray, yes, but I also spend hours consumed by the problem. I think it through from all angles, I craft and plot solutions and ways of getting out of whatever the mess is.

I become totally problem-centered; I become the hungry hunter sitting on a log, bow in hand, staring at my rumbling belly.

When you are faced with a problem and you begin to pray it through, think about that hungry hunter. Understand where the answers to your problems are. Jesus is the answer for every problem, every lack; everything you need is available in Him.

Focusing on your need is like feeding fresh kindling to a fire. It fuels all the worries and doubts, the concerns and fears. But when you focus on the source of all solutions—Jesus—you draw on His limitless resources to provide for you, protect you, or solve the problem. To focus on the source of your solution is to reach for the bucket of sand that will kill the fire.

So when you start praying, be like that hunter. Focus on the solution to your need: Jesus. He is the complete answer to anything that you are facing.

Now, I'm not suggesting we stop thinking. God has given us good brains and logic for a reason. The trouble comes when we exclude Him from our thinking and only look to ourselves to untie the knotty mess of our circumstances.

He is waiting for you to look to Him to be enough for whatever situation you are facing. He is your *more than enough.*

~ Thought for the Day ~

What problems are taking up your focus right now?

 Dear Lord, please will You remind me of the hunter staring at his belly each time I become problem-focused instead of Jesus-focused.

5

Two Sides of the Screen

"For my thoughts are not your thoughts,
Neither are your ways my ways," declares the Lord.
"As the heavens are higher than the earth,
So are my ways higher than your ways
And my thoughts than your thoughts."
(Isaiah 55:8-9)

Have you ever been to a drive-in movie? With technology bringing movie theaters into our homes, drive-in movies are all but extinct, but it sure was fun while it lasted.

For those of you who never got to go, it worked like this: You paid to drive into a big lot and everyone parked their cars facing the huge screen. You hooked a speaker onto your window and, voila!, you got to watch a movie from the comfort of your own car. The sound quality was terrible, but you could fall asleep quite comfortably if the movie was boring. You could bring your own snacks or there was a shop onsite if you wanted to go buy some nibbles.

It was a great outing for a family back in the day.

Only the cars who paid at the entrance were allowed into the fenced off area in front of the screen. There was this one time we didn't have money to pay to go in. So we parked outside the drive-in behind the screen and tried to listen to the movie from there. Listening to the movie without any clue what was happening on screen was not the best idea. (Who was screaming and why? What were they all laughing at?)

I had a similar experience in church one morning. We sang a song that has two very different meanings depending on where you place the emphasis. It was almost like watching a movie from two different sides of the screen.

*I see a generation **breaking** through despair.*

I read this and saw broken people, hopeless and trashed.

*I see a generation breaking **through** despair.*

Aah, a triumphant generation! Smashing through despair before lunch.

When life hands you a challenge, there are always two ways of looking at it. The enemy is too subtle to change the facts, but he does shift the emphasis. If we look at our lives through his perspective, things can seem grim.

But when we park off next to God and allow Him to show us what is going on from His perspective, things look a whole lot different. The facts may be the same—the diagnosis, the test score, the bank balance— but your loving Heavenly Father is more than able to take care of you when you put your trust in Him.

Is it possible for you to switch to a different perspective? Those who believe in positive thinking will say yes. But trusting God with your life is way deeper than positive thinking. Trusting Him means being able to say, "Lord, I want to trust You, but I'm not able to. Please change my thinking."

As you yield to Him in whatever small way you can, He will enable you to trust Him more and you will grow in that trust. Yield your mind to Him and allow Him to renew it!

As He shifts things on the inside, you'll find yourself parked in front of the screen of His grace, watching Him working in your life in all the glorious technicolor you could ever imagine!

~ Thought for the Day ~

Are you willing to let God change your ability to trust Him for the things that you are asking him for?

Is yielding, or surrendering, to Him hard for you?

 Dear Lord, I ask for Your perspective and 'right emphasis' on every trouble I face. Help me always to see that I have front row seats to Your miracles.

6

The Soundtrack of Your Mind

"Peace I leave with you; my peace I give you. I do not give to you as the world gives. Do not let your hearts be troubled and do not be afraid."
(John 14:27)

Call me a ninny, but I don't like watching horror movies or thrillers. As a kid with my wild imagination, watching anything scary was like inviting all those characters to come live in my head and keep me from sleeping with the light off for weeks.

I was about nine years old and we were in the middle of an old movie about giant ants and I wasn't coping. The ants were doing something boring like crossing a grassy patch, they weren't even doing anything scary, but I couldn't deal with them. My mom, being the clever woman she was, told me to block my ears.

I thought she was completely nuts, but I had nothing to lose. I popped a finger in each ear and the strangest thing happened. The moment I couldn't hear the soundtrack, what was happening on the screen wasn't all that scary anymore. In fact, the ants seemed funny.

What made the difference? The soundtrack playing in my head.

The music they'd chosen to accompany the ants across the grass was menacing and it worked. It turned something comical into something terrifying.

It works on little girls with vivid imaginations, but here's the thing—it works on grown-ups too and it doesn't always come in the form of music, but rather in the form of thoughts. With the world in the mess it's in, it doesn't take much to allow our thoughts to be toxic.

As you go through your day, pay attention to the soundtrack that is playing in your mind. See if you can catch some of your thoughts as they roll off your tongue.

If your thoughts leave you scared, worried, unsettled, anxious, or sad, then you can be sure it isn't the whisper of the Holy Spirit you're listening to. It is time to change tracks.

Without you being consciously aware of it, you might find your mental soundtrack runs a non-stop playlist of fear, concerns, and worries—both real and imagined.

With that running over and over in the background of your mind, you'll find even the most harmless situations and conversations take on a sinister edge.

For little girls and scary movies, fingers in ears work beautifully, but as an adult how do you go about changing how you think?

Thought patterns can create ruts in your mind that train your brain to think in a particular way. Changing your mental soundtrack isn't impossible, especially when God gets involved.

Make a point of checking your thoughts every so often. When you're sitting in traffic, what are thinking? In the shower. Cooking supper. Take note of your thoughts, jot them down if you need to. If you see an unhealthy pattern, here are some ways to bring them back into line:

• Speak to God about your thoughts. Ask Him to renew your mind.

• Read your Bible more regularly.

• Practice memorizing scriptures. This will keep your mind busy and retrain your thoughts.

• If you catch gloomy thoughts, actively oppose them. Ask yourself, what does God say about this? Find a verse to counter the glooms and purposefully focus on it.

• For some folks, listening to worship music will help.

Awareness is half the battle won. Allow God to soak you in His love and truth and watch your mind change tracks to the soundtrack of Heaven!

~ Thought for the Day ~

What is on your mental playlist?

What method of changing tracks in your mind will work best for you?

Dear Lord, I understand how powerful thoughts are. I ask You to guard my heart and mind with Your Truth. Thank you!

7

Influencer, Not Influenced

"The light shines in the darkness, and the darkness has not overcome it."
(John 1:5)

If you take a stroll through swampy, muddy water, by the time you make it out the other side, your clothes will be soggy and stained. You'll probably smell bad, too, and have picked up a couple of leeches.

Now imagine if there were such a thing as swamp transformation spray. Not just a repellent, but a transforming agent. You would spray it on liberally and as you walked through a swamp, not only would the dirty water not affect you, but you'd leave a trail of clear, clean water in your wake. That would be quite something.

Friend, this is the potency of the Spirit Life of God that we carry inside.

I used to love watching those medical movies where there's an outbreak of a highly contagious disease. It was quite surreal to see it play out in real life on a global stage in 2020.

Just like in the movies, we watched medical professionals roll into town in their bio-hazard suits and set up temporary lab facilities to diagnose and treat the symptoms of the super-virus.

To me, that is a perfect picture of us as spiritual beings in the natural world. The medical people don't stay away from the outbreak for fear of being contaminated. On the contrary, they head straight into the thick of it.

But do they head in unprotected? Not at all. Each one is carefully sealed inside their bio-hazard suit, untouchable by the killer virus.

When it comes to us being light to people stuck in spiritual darkness, Jesus is our "bio-hazard suit" that makes it possible for us to hang out with people who don't yet believe what we do, don't live as "clean" as we try to, and don't yet know how much God loves them.

This is nothing to do with Corona, masks and hand sanitizer, and everything to do with our love for sinners. Jesus was always found with those that society shunned as unclean, so much so, that He offended the religious leaders of the day.

Hidden safely in Jesus, we do not need to hide away from broken, hurting people for fear of being influenced. We can become the Influencers that God created us to be.

The world is a harsh place and people are struggling. Nobody has been untouched by all that 2020 has thrown at us. Is this the time for us to shrink back, batten down the hatches, and try our best to survive? Do we withdraw from the challenges facing our people? Or do we follow Jesus' example and LIVE, allowing God's transforming love to pour through us as far as we go in spite of the harshness of life?

It's overwhelming to look at the tremendous brokenness all around us. I find myself shutting it out because it's all too much to process. How could we make a difference to anyone in this mess?

And yet, as we climb onto Jesus' lap and put our ears to His chest, we'll begin to live in time to the beating of His heart. As we do that, I suspect He'll show us one thing, just one thing, that we can do. When that's done, there'll be one more.

As we take up the challenge of bearing His light in this dark world, it will be His transforming power that will bring healing and hope as we go where He tells us, and do what He shows us.

Faced with a broken, dark world, there's not much we can do in our own strength to bring relief and help. But when He leads and we follow, dear friend, we can bring His Life, His Hope and His Healing to many. We can bring His Light to the darkness.

~ Thought for the Day ~

Do you see yourself as an influencer, or one who is being influenced?

Dear Lord, as I grow into being the influencer You're calling me to be, would you open my eyes to those things that influence me and sway my heart so easily? Thank You Lord that no matter what life sends my way, I know I can face it with You. Make me a beacon of hope that points to You at all times. Thank You!

About Dianne J. Wilson

Weaving Invisible into Words

Dianne J. Wilson writes across genres including Humor, Women's Fiction, Romantic Suspense, and YA Fantasy. Weaving Invisible into words, she explores spiritual truth woven through ordinary life with equal dashes of breathless adventure and tongue-in-cheek humor, all soaked in God's Grace. She writes in stolen moments, usually in the back seat of her tiny car. Her home is in East London, a South African coastal town, where she lives with her hubby and three daughters who all take turns at being home.

Her love-language is tea and taking long drives to listen to new songs with her girls. When she's not stuck in her car writing, you can find her feeding all the hungry people in her house who gaze at her expectantly around mealtimes.

Please visit Dianne's website for more of her books:
www.diannejwilson.com

Email Dianne: diannejenniferwilson@gmail.com

Titles by Dianne J. Wilson

CONTEMPORARY WOMEN'S FICTION
THE LIST BOOKS
Order, Chaos and The Grace In Between

The Cake List
A Shopping List Of Noes *(releasing 2020)*

INSPIRATIONAL SMALL TOWN ROM-COM
RIVER VALLEY ROMANCE

No Cows, Please
No Chefs, Please (releasing 2021)

CHRISTIAN ROMANTIC SUSPENSE

Shackles
Finding Mia

TEEN/YA URBAN FANTASY
THE SPIRIT WALKER TRILOGY

Affinity *(Book 1)*
Resonance *(Book 2)*
Cadence *(Book 3)*

Seven Saints in
LOCKDOWN

How they became
Overcomers

Val Waldeck

SEVEN SAINTS IN LOCKDOWN

Table of Contents

Introduction

2020 will be remembered as the year of the Covid-19 Virus that plunged the entire global community into a state of chaos and fear.

Most of the world's citizens found themselves in a lockdown position. Residents of South Africa were considered to have experienced one of the strictest lockdown regimes in the world.

Months of being strictly regulated led to economic hardship for many. Some businesses never recovered. Social distancing, strict hygiene protocols, and mandatory wearing of masks added to the stress of trying to live a normal life.

Some people have expressed a wish to move to a desert island and live there all by themselves. The lockdown experience gave a whole new dimension to that thought. People did *not* enjoy being separated from their family and peers.

Many suffered what has been called Lockdown Fatigue. Psychologists say the foggy thinking and difficulty concentrating is due to our brains over-processing all the new experiences and ways of doing things. The uncertainty of the times has caused stress and impaired thinking, and many people became depressed as a result. Some even committed suicide.

Christians are not immune to this kind of negative impact, but the good news is there is an answer to this dilemma. We can be overcomers despite our circumstances.

We are going to follow seven Old Testament believers who experienced lockdown during their lifetimes. They were overcomers and teach us the secret of victorious living. In each case, we will notice two major factors in their lives. They kept in close contact with the Lord and believed His Word despite their circumstances.

Get ready for an exciting journey through the Bible. It could change your life.

Val Waldeck
Durban, South Africa.
www.valwaldeck.com

1

Job

"But as for me, I know that my Redeemer lives."
(Job 19:25)

How often we cry out, *"I can't take it!"* when the storms of life rise and threaten to destroy us. We forget so quickly the principles we have learned through life's many experiences as our stress levels rise. Lockdown has had this effect on many people.

The Old Testament book of Job tells us about a man who suffered a terrible loss. Job came through the storm with his faith intact as he triumphed over sin, sickness, and death. His wife came through the same storm, but she fell apart emotionally and spiritually on her journey back to faith.

Attitude made the difference. It always makes a difference as to *how* we weather our storms.

Many scholars believe Job was a contemporary of Abraham and the book written about him is certainly one of the oldest in the Bible. He lived in the Middle East and was a well-known and respected figure in his community. Job was a rich man. He had a large family, a huge staff, and many possessions.

But in one day Job lost his entire staff, except for three men. He also lost his business and all the capital he had invested in livestock. He was bankrupt.

While Job was trying to come to terms with his loss, he was informed his ten beloved children – whom he prayed for every morning without fail – had died in a terrible accident.

Then he lost his health and found himself in lockdown in the village dump. Covered in painful sores and at the point of death, people were afraid to come near him. His wife urged him to commit suicide. "Curse God and die!" this bitter disillusioned woman told her husband. His wealth was lost, his home was gone, his precious children were dead, and he was in a gross physical state. What was there left to live for?

But Job was an overcomer and he kept a positive attitude. Here are seven things we can learn from him.

1. Job acknowledged God's sovereignty. *"The LORD gave, and the LORD has taken away,"* he insisted. (Job 1:21)

2. Job refused to allow the "root of bitterness" to enter his heart (Hebrews 12:15*). "Blessed be the name of the LORD,"* he said. (Job 1:22)

3. Job worshipped God and bowed down to His Lordship. If the sovereign Lord had allowed this, it was good enough for Job. *"Shall we indeed accept good from God, and shall we not accept adversity?"* he asked. (Job 2:10)

4. Job exercised his faith and believed God would make a way. *"Though He slay me, yet will I trust Him,"* he insisted. (Job 13:15)

243

5. Job was prepared to learn from his trial. He believed once the Lord had tested the reality of his faith, only what was spurious would be blown away and gold would be left. *"But He knows the way that I take; When He has tested me, I shall come forth as gold,"* he testified. (Job 23:10)

6. Job had a long-term view of life. What happens on this earth is preparation for a life of eternal joy in the presence of God for those who know the Savior, the Lord Jesus Christ. No matter what happens to us, its value lasts for a moment in the light of eternity. *"For I know that my Redeemer lives,"* Job insisted. (Job 19:25-27)

7. Job refused to be influenced by his wife or his friends. When he needed her the most, his wife spoke words of death to him. His friends accused him of secret sin, deserving the wrath of God. Job stood firm. He believed God even when things looked their bleakest.

The end of the story is a happy one. God is faithful, even when we are not (2 Timothy 2:13), and he brought both Job and his wife safely through the trial. He restored to them double of everything they had lost. (Job 42:10-17)

A poignant moment in this story of God's faithfulness is the comment about Job's children. God gave them ten more children, a wonderful assurance to Job that his prayers were answered, and he had double the number of children indeed – ten in heaven and ten on earth. (Job 42:13)

God is faithful, sovereign, and kind. He is sufficient for any storm or lockdown. When we choose to believe that and stand firm in our faith as Job did, we will find that we too can "take it" in His strength and by His

Grace. That is the attitude of an overcomer.

Can you view your present circumstances like Job? Are you prepared to believe God is sovereign and everything is under control, even if it does not look that way? This is the secret to becoming an overcomer.

Here is a Word of encouragement for you.
Turn it into your personal prayer.

"The temptations in your life are no different
from what others experience.
And God is faithful.
He will not allow the temptation to be
more than you can stand.
When you are tempted, he will show you a way out
so that you can endure."
(1 Corinthians 10:13)

2

Moses

*"Then Moses raised his hand over the sea, and the Lord opened up a path
through the water with a strong east wind. The wind blew all that night, turning
the seabed into dry land."*
(Exodus 14:21)

Moses and the Israelites were in a serious lockdown situation. He had
just led three to four million Israelites out of Egypt. That is a lot of
people! If they had today's transport available, it would have taken at
least 80,000 tourist buses just to carry the people. Their luggage and
supplies would have required another two freight trains, each at least a
mile long.

Moses was an educated man. He was no fool, but the logistics didn't give
him sleepless nights. He had spent 40 years in Egypt as the Pharaoh's
adopted son, thinking he was a Somebody; 40 years in the desert coming
to the realization he was a Nobody, and 40 years in the Wilderness
experiencing that God was the All-Sufficient One. He knew God would
take care of the details. All he had to do was trust and obey.

They were on their way to the Promised Land when they heard Pharaoh
had changed his mind and sent his army to capture them. The situation
looked impossible to the Israelites as they stood on the shores of the Red
Sea.

Behind them came the powerful army of Egypt. In front of them stood the sea. There was nowhere to go, and human wisdom had no answer. And worse, a strong east wind blew all night to add to their misery. The sand got in their eyes, their noses, their ears. What else could go wrong? It looked like there was no hope.

Are you in that situation today... in your life, your marriage, your job? You don't know where to turn or what to do. You cannot go backward or forward as the strong winds of circumstances buffet you. Will you trust the Lord with your problem and resolve to obey His direction?

Moses trusted the Lord to make a way and He did. The wind causing them so much discomfort was the very instrument God used to blow a path through the waters. That is the reason it had to be a *strong* wind!

Moses told the people to stand still.

"Don't be afraid. Just stand still
and watch the LORD rescue you today.
The Egyptians you see today will never be seen again.
The LORD himself will fight for you.
Just stay calm."

(Exodus 14:13-14)

That is good advice, but the truth is we also need to obey God and do the possible. Then *He* will do the impossible. There is no point in just sitting still and waiting for something to happen. We need to be still only to hear the Voice of God, and then we must get moving.

That is what God told Moses to tell the people. *"Then the LORD said to Moses, 'Why are you crying*

247

out to me? Tell the people to get moving!
Pick up your staff and raise your hand over the sea.
Divide the water so the Israelites can walk
through the middle of the sea on dry ground."'

(Exodus 14:15-16)

Moses obeyed the Lord and by faith, the people of Israel walked through the middle of the sea on dry ground, with walls of water on each side!

There is a big difference between faith based on the Word of God, and presumption. The Egyptian armies tried the same thing with disastrous results.

What made Moses an overcomer? Simply hearing, believing, and acting on the inspired Word of God. That will make you and me overcomers too.

Why not kneel on the shores of your Red Sea and acknowledge His sovereignty in the strong east wind blowing in your life?

Allow the Lord Jesus Christ to help you "*His way*" as you faithfully obey the leading of the Holy Spirit.

 Turn this powerful Scripture into your personal prayer.
"Trust in the LORD with all your heart;
do not depend on your own understanding.
Seek his will in all you do,
and he will show you which path to take."

(Proverbs 3:5-6)

3

Joseph

"You intended to harm me, but God intended it all for good. He brought me to
this position so I could
save the lives of many people."
(Genesis 50:20)

Joseph was the son of Jacob, grandson of Isaac, and great-grandson of
Abraham. His family loved the Lord and God had His hand on this
young man. But he had some issues in his life. Times of lockdown were
necessary to deal with them so he could fulfill his purpose.

Young Joseph loved to tell tales about his brothers to their father. It made
them angry. He was already acknowledged as Jacob's favorite son and
they were green with envy. His special coat made them see red. It's a
colorful story.

When they saw him coming to check on them once again, he experienced
his first lockdown. They put him in a pit and sold him to a band of
travelers. Once they reached Egypt, he was sold to an Egyptian citizen as
a slave. Potiphar's wife attempted unsuccessfully to seduce him, and
Joseph landed up in prison falsely accused of attempted rape. His story is
told in Genesis chapters 37-50.

Joseph discovered the secret of victory during lockdown was to keep in close touch with the Lord. His trust in God and a good attitude made life in slavery easier.

The Lord taught him management skills and he rose to prominence in Potiphar's employ. Imprisoned on false charges, Joseph kept his focus on the Lord. Once again, his attitude brought him favor.

Many times, he must have longed for the freedom to live a normal life again. Are you feeling that way today? Meditate on the fact that God used these lockdown experiences to prepare him for the purpose he was born to achieve. He was destined to become second-in-command to Pharaoh himself and oversee a feeding program that would save people from starvation and death. More than that, his purpose included saving his family and paving the way for Messiah to be born years later. Our lives affect more people than we realize.

The Apostle Paul suffered times of lockdown too and he testified:

"I have learned how to be content with whatever I have.
I know how to live on almost nothing or with everything.
I have learned the secret of living in every situation, whether it is with a
full stomach or empty,
with plenty or little.
For I can do everything through Christ, who gives me strength."

(Philippians 4:11-13)

God loves us dearly, but He loves us too much to leave us as we are. Even when Joseph rose to a position of power and authority in Egypt, the Lord was not finished with him yet.

Many have seen him as a type of Christ, but he certainly was not perfect. You've heard of the elephant in the room? This godly man had an issue in his life that needed to be dealt with.

People were starving all over the known world and Joseph knew that. He also knew his beloved father, mother, and brothers were in need. Yet he did not attempt to assist them, even though he could.

When his brothers came looking for grain, he treated them roughly and imprisoned them on false charges. Egyptian prisons were not a lot of fun. Why did he behave like this? It seems unforgiveness for childhood issues lurked deep in his heart.

It took a while before his attitude melted and he acknowledged his family. Reconciliation was a wonderful experience for them, and Joseph took on the responsibility of caring for his aged father and brothers.

The Bible tells us that "those who won't care for their relatives, especially those in their own household, have denied the true faith. Such people are worse than unbelievers" (1 Timothy 5:8).

Joseph believed in the sovereignty of God. His brothers may have been responsible for sending him to Egypt, but God used those circumstances to bring about His perfect will for Joseph's life.

The scriptures assure us "that God causes everything to work together for the good of those who love God and are called according to his purpose for them" (Romans 8:28).

Had Joseph become bitter and angry, he may have lost touch with God and wasted his life. They intended evil, but God intended good.

Are you having issues with your family, relatives, friends, colleagues, and neighbors? It could be a major factor hindering your recovery from the adverse effects of lockdown. Make the decision today to forgive and let it go.

We have all been forgiven by the Lord for so much. We can choose to forgive because we have been forgiven.

"Make allowance for each other's faults,
and forgive anyone who offends you.
Remember, the Lord forgave you,
so you must forgive others."

(Colossians 3:13)

This is the way to become an overcomer like Joseph.

––––––––––––––

 Turn this powerful Scripture into your personal prayer:
"...forgive us our sins,
as we have forgiven those who sin against us."
(Matthew 6:12)

4

Elijah

"Elijah was as human as we are, and yet when he prayed earnestly that no rain would fall, none fell for three and a half years! Then, when he prayed again, the sky sent down rain and the earth began to yield its crops."
(James 5:17-18)

Elijah was a powerful 8th Century BC prophet. He fearlessly proclaimed the Word of God and ended up in lockdown situations quite often as a result. He was not afraid to stand up for truth, no matter the cost. Elijah challenged kings and leaders, men and women, without fear or favor. This was a man who knew how to pray.

We understand in this generation how difficult it is to speak out about immorality, sin, and unbiblical behavior. The reaction of people and groups is often violent and has serious consequences. Many believers prefer to just pray. Few speak out boldly, despite possible consequences. Elijah in his generation was one of those few.

On one occasion he was forced to take refuge at the Kerith Brook near the Jordan River. King Ahab was determined to kill him. This prophet was an overcomer in lockdown. He had no fear of man and knew his God. While at the brook, the Lord used ravens to feed him morning and evening.

Later he took refuge at a widow's home in the village of Zarephath. She was extremely poor and about to eat her last meal with her son. "I was just gathering a few sticks to cook this last meal, and then my son and I will die" she told him.

> *"Don't be afraid!" Elijah responded.*
> *"Go ahead and do just what you've said*
> *but make a little bread for me first.*
> *Then use what's left to prepare a meal*
> *for yourself and your son."*

(1 Kings 17:12-13)

To her surprise, there was always enough flour and olive oil left in the container, just as the Lord had promised through Elijah.

Elijah had a successful and powerful ministry, but there came a time when life just seemed too much for him. He challenged the 450 prophets of Baal to build an altar on Mount Carmel and offer a sacrifice.

"Call on the name of your god," he shouted, "and I will call on the name of the LORD. The god who answers by setting fire to the wood is the true God!" (1 Kings 18:24)

Those prophets shouted and danced, they cut themselves with knives and swords and performed all day, but there was no response from their gods.

Elijah poured water on his sacrifice. He dug a trench around the altar and poured about nine gallons of water into it. Then he prayed.

The fire of God came down from heaven, burned up the sacrifice, the altar, and evaporated the water. When all the people saw it, they fell face down on the ground and cried out, "The LORD—he is God! Yes, the LORD is God!" (1 Kings 18:39).

Jezebel, the wife of King Ahab, was furious and threatened to kill Elijah. In a moment of emotional weakness, this great prophet ran for his life.

Elijah found himself in lockdown again, this time under a broom tree in the wilderness. He felt suicidal and prayed to die. He had no more strength.

The Lord sent an angel with bread and water. Elijah ate and lay down again.

"Then the angel of the LORD came again and touched him and said, 'Get up and eat some more, or the journey ahead will be too much for you.' So he got up and ate and drank, and the food gave him enough strength to travel forty days and forty nights to Mount Sinai, the mountain of God."

(1 Kings 19:7-8)

It was there in a cave he met with God and heard that still, small voice. A short while later, the Lord sent a chariot of fire and Elijah was caught up into heaven. Had he died earlier, he would never have had that marvelous experience.

Very often, after a huge event or successful ministry, we feel "flat" and tired. The rush of adrenaline subsides and leaves us weak. Perhaps you are feeling that kind of burnout right now. It closely resembles the well-known symptom called Lockdown Fatigue. The Bible tells us Jesus always prayed before and after events. He knew how to combat burnout.

Here is the secret of the Overcomer. Feed on the Bread of Life and Drink at the Fountain of Living Water. Take time out to read the Word of God and meditate on the promises and principles of God. Pray them into your spirit. You will find strength enough for your journey and experience the wonderful presence of God.

Christian, keep on keeping on! Never, never, never give up or give in.

 Turn this powerful Scripture into your personal prayer:
"He gives power to the weak
and strength to the powerless.
Even youths will become weak and tired,
and young men will fall in exhaustion.
But those who trust in the LORD will find new strength.
They will soar high on wings like eagles.
They will run and not grow weary.
They will walk and not faint."
(Isaiah 40:29-31)

5

Jeremiah

"I knew you before I formed you in your mother's womb. Before you were born I set you apart and appointed you as my prophet to the nations."
(Jeremiah 1:5)

Jeremiah had a problem. He loved the Lord and desired to fulfill his calling, but it wasn't easy. He lived around 600 BC. Israel was divided into two kingdoms at the time. The Northern kingdom, consisting of ten tribes had been conquered by the Assyrians. The Southern Kingdom, comprising the tribes of Judah and Benjamin (Israel as we know it today) was in serious trouble with God. Their idolatry and immorality had reached a crisis point and the Lord called Jeremiah to warn them. Unless they repented, the Babylonians would soon invade them.

Jeremiah knew this message would not go down well. At first, he tried to get out of his assignment. "O Sovereign Lord, I can't speak for You. I'm too young," he said (Jeremiah 1:6).

Has the Lord called you to do something for Him? Are you making excuses? Are you reluctant to obey because it may bring trouble and persecution your way?

The Lord is not impressed by excuses.

"Don't say, 'I'm too young,' for you must go wherever I send you and say

whatever I tell you. And don't be afraid of the people, for I will be with
you and will protect you. I, the LORD, have spoken!"

(Jeremiah 1:7-8)

Jeremiah was about to learn how to become an overcomer in adverse times. He somewhat reluctantly spoke out against evil and sure enough, trouble came his way. He complained to the Lord. He was shocked at what the Lord had to say.

"If racing against mere men makes you tired,
how will you race against horses?"

(Jeremiah 12:5)

If we can't handle minor persecution, how will we stand when we face severe trouble? The writer of the book of Hebrews presents us with the same challenge. *"Think of all the hostility he [Jesus] endured from sinful people; then you won't become weary and give up. After all, you have not yet given your lives in your struggle against sin."*

(Hebrews 12:3-4)

Jeremiah accepted the challenge and continued his ministry as a prophet, speaking on behalf of the Lord to a rebellious people. But things got even worse. They became so angry with him, he was whipped and put in stocks. A stock is a wooden or metal device with holes for securing the head, hands, and feet. Placed in a public area, the victim is at the mercy of the crowds.

It was not a good place to be and Jeremiah was angry. "I wish I had never been born," he muttered. He vowed never to mention the Lord or speak in His Name again. But he couldn't keep that up for long.

"His words burn in my heart like a fire…
I can't do it!"
(Jeremiah 20:9)

At last, he focused on the Lord who promised to stand by him. That is the secret to being an overcomer. When we turn our eyes away from our problems and focus on Jesus, everything changes.

"The Lord stands beside me like a great warrior," he wrote (Jeremiah 20:11). With Him at his side, Jeremiah knew he could face anything. The man became an overcomer the moment he believed and received the promises of God. That was his secret and it is ours too.

The Word of God gives us the courage to stand firm, no matter what is happening around us.

It wasn't long before Jeremiah found himself in an even worse situation. They lowered him into a deep smelly pit with ropes and left him to die (Jeremiah chapter 38).

This was lockdown at its worst. Did Jeremiah lose faith again and question God's goodness?

This man had become an overcomer and there was no word of complaint. Soon the Lord moved upon the officials to take him out of the pit.

Judah was conquered, and we hear no more about Jeremiah. He had faithfully fulfilled his mission and his eternal reward awaited him.

What can we take away from the story of this great Man of God? Just this, God is faithful. Trust Him no matter what it costs.

He is more than able to keep and strengthen you in your journey of faith. Keep speaking for Him. Do not be silent. Let your voice be heard.

Your reward will far outweigh the discomfort you may be suffering now.

 Turn this powerful Scripture into your personal prayer:

"Now to Him who is able to keep you from stumbling,
And to present you faultless
before the presence of His glory with exceeding joy,
To God our Savior, Who alone is wise,
Be glory and majesty, Dominion and power,
Both now and forever.
Amen."
(Jude 1:24-25)

6

Shadrach, Meshach, and Abednego

"If we are thrown into the blazing furnace, the God whom we serve is able to save us. He will rescue us from your power, Your Majesty. But even if he doesn't, we want to make it clear to you, Your Majesty, that we will never serve your gods or worship the gold statue you have set up."
(Daniel 3:17-18)

Have you ever felt as though you were in circumstances that seemed to be like a fiery furnace? The heat was on and there was no way out. You felt sure you would be destroyed emotionally and perhaps even physically.

Let me share with you today about three Hebrew young men. For the purposes of this book, I have looked on them as one entity, although they were three men.

They were captives from Israel, together with Daniel. Locked down in Babylon was not their first choice, but no doubt inspired by Daniel, they kept their eyes on the Lord. These men maintained a positive attitude, despite their circumstances. They understood God is sovereign and were prepared to entrust the outcome to Him.

Whether they lived to tell the tale, or whether they transferred to Glory, they had nothing to lose.

Daniel had earlier interpreted King Nebuchadnezzar's dream about a huge statue. It represented the five final world empires leading to the end of world history as we know it. The details are recorded in Daniel chapter 2.

Nebuchadnezzar was impressed, but he couldn't help thinking about the fact that the head of the statue represented *his* kingdom, Babylon. He felt important.

Soon the idea came into his head to build a golden statue just like the one in his dream. It stood nine-feet tall and he commanded everyone to bow down and worship it when the music played. Failure to bow the knee to the latest political philosophy invited serious persecution and death.

History does have a way of repeating itself, doesn't it? What is your response to organizations that are fundamentally anti-Christian in their ethos and methods but demand you bow the knee? Every Christian needs to question whether they are supporting a political cause because of pressure, or whether they prefer to reserve the act of bowing the knee as a sign of adoration, confession, humility, and worship before Almighty God. He loves people equally and made them of "one blood" (Acts 17:26).

Shadrach, Meshach, and Abednego did not waver for a moment. They stood tall when everyone else capitulated. They were prepared to pay the price.

The king was white-hot with anger. He ordered the three men to change their minds and bow down.

"I will give you one more chance to bow down and worship the statue I have made when you hear the sound of the musical instruments. But if you refuse, you will be thrown immediately into the blazing furnace. And then what god will be able to rescue you from my power?"

(Daniel 3:15)

Many people have faced this situation in our day. Some have bowed the knee to the applause of the crowd. Others have stood firm and suffered serious consequences, losing much in the process. What would these young men do?

Without hesitation, they replied:

"O Nebuchadnezzar, we do not need to
defend ourselves before you.
If we are thrown into the blazing furnace,
the God whom we serve is able to save us.
He will rescue us from your power, Your Majesty.
But even if he doesn't, we want to make it clear to you,
Your Majesty, that we will never serve your gods
or worship the gold statue you have set up."

(Daniel 3:16-18)

They were prepared to burn, but never to bow to anyone but the Living God.

Nebuchadnezzar was so angry, he ordered the furnace heated seven times hotter than usual. The heat was so intense, the flames killed the soldiers as they securely tied up the three men and then threw them into the burning fiery furnace. How could they possibly survive?

263

When the king looked into the furnace, he saw four men walking around in the flames. Nebuchadnezzar jumped up in amazement and exclaimed to his advisers, "Didn't we tie up three men and throw them into the furnace?"

"Yes, Your Majesty, we certainly did," they replied.

"Look!" Nebuchadnezzar shouted. "I see four men, unbound, walking around in the fire unharmed! And the fourth looks like a god!" (Daniel 3:24-25).

"Come out," he ordered. So Shadrach, Meshach, and Abednego stepped out of the fire.

"Then the high officers, officials, governors, and advisers crowded around them and saw the fire had not touched them. Not a hair on their heads was singed, and their clothing was not scorched. They didn't even smell of smoke!"

(Daniel 3:26-27)

The king promoted Shadrach, Meshach, and Abednego to even higher positions in the province of Babylon. God always honors those who honor Him.

Our sovereign God can deliver us from the hottest situations. Stop for a moment and wait on the Lord with your problem. The Lord has the solution and the fire will not destroy you.

"You are of God, little children, and have overcome them, because He who is in you is greater than he who is in the world."

(1 John 4:4)

Turn this powerful Scripture into your personal prayer:

"When you go through deep waters,

I will be with you.

When you go through rivers of difficulty,

you will not drown.

When you walk through the fire of oppression,

you will not be burned up;

the flames will not consume you.

For I am the LORD, your God,

the Holy One of Israel, your Savior."

(Isaiah 43:2-3)

7

Daniel

"But when Daniel learned that the law had been signed, he went home and knelt down as usual in his upstairs room, with its windows open toward Jerusalem. He prayed three times a day, just as he had always done, giving thanks to his God."
(Daniel 6:10)

Daniel crosses our path today as a breath of fresh air. This man came from a godly family and he knew how to pray and listen to God. He was an overcomer.

As a young boy, Daniel was taken into captivity by the Babylonians when they invaded Judah, just as Jeremiah had prophesied. In exile, he continued to pore over Jeremiah's writings and believed God's promise that his nation would return to their land after 70 years.

Daniel kept his eyes on the Lord. When he rose to prominence in the Babylonian court, and later in the Persian government, he never stopped praying and worshipping God. His time in lockdown was not wasted.

His enemies hated the fact that a Jew was senior leader in their country (Daniel 6:3). They especially disliked that he was a man of integrity. No one could bribe him or corrupt his convictions. He stood firmly on the Word of God and kept in daily contact with his Lord. This was a man who prayed consistently three times a day and listened to the Lord carefully.

The Book of Daniel in the Old Testament contains the most detailed prophesies of the End Times in existence. God shared many things with this believer who was never too busy to listen.

The Lord shared His prophetic blueprint for the world with Daniel. He told him about the five great empires that would rule the world before the Second Coming of Messiah – Babylon, Persia, Greece, Rome, and the Revived Roman Empire led by the antichrist.

There is even specific detail in his book about the timing of Christ's first coming, His death, resurrection, and return.

Remember, he lived around 600 BC. We are living thousands of years later and watching these prophecies come to pass with precision.

Daniel experienced a lockdown of a kind you and I would never want to share. His enemies tricked the king into signing a decree stating that he alone should be worshipped for 30 days on penalty of death. Daniel was unperturbed.

"But when Daniel learned that the law had been signed, he went home and knelt down as usual in his upstairs room, with its windows open toward Jerusalem. He prayed three times a day, just as he had always done, giving thanks to his God."

(Daniel 6:10)

This was a man who knew the God he spent quality time with daily. He was fully convinced God is sovereign and anything He allows in our lives is for a good purpose.

He knew what lay ahead. A den of hungry lions where people who displeased the king or his officials ended up. Before the victims even reached the bottom of the pit, those lions fiercely tore them apart. There was no fire escape. He looked down at the snarling lions and worshipped as he was tossed into the den of lions.

"Very early the next morning, the king got up and hurried out to the lions' den. When he got there, he called out in anguish, 'Daniel, servant of the living God! Was your God, whom you serve so faithfully, able to rescue you from the lions?'"

(Daniel 6:19-20)

God had given the lions lockjaw! Daniel had a peaceful sleep that night. Maybe he even used one of the lions as a pillow.

"My God sent his angel to shut the lions' mouths so that they would not hurt me, for I have been found innocent in his sight. And I have not wronged you, Your Majesty," he replied.

The king was overjoyed and ordered that Daniel be lifted from the den. Not a scratch was found on him, for he had trusted in his God.

When we trust God with the outcome of our lockdown experience, we find *He* is not locked down. He is more than able to meet us at our point of need.

Daniel is an inspiring example. He never suffered from the lockdown syndrome because he spent time with God, no matter the circumstances.

Three things stand out about Daniel's life. He was a man who prayed consistently, searched the scriptures, and was able to endure persecution as a result.

These things made Daniel an overcomer.

 Turn this powerful Scripture into your personal prayer:

"Oh, the joys of those who do not
follow the advice of the wicked,
or stand around with sinners,
or join in with mockers.
But they delight in the law of the LORD,
meditating on it day and night.
They are like trees planted along the riverbank,
bearing fruit each season.
Their leaves never wither,
and they prosper in all they do."
(Psalm 1:1-3)

The Overcomer's Secret

Years ago, Sunday School children were taught the Overcomer's Secret in a short song. It went like this:

Read Your Bible

Pray Every Day

And You Will Grow… Grow… Grow

Those words are as relevant today as they were in times past.

Those who desire to become overcomers in our generation will do well to follow this simple advice given to Joshua by Moses.

"Study this Book of Instruction continually. Meditate on it day and night so you will be sure to obey everything written in it. Only then will you prosper and succeed in all you do. This is my command—be strong and courageous! Do not be afraid or discouraged. For the LORD your God is with you wherever you go."

(Joshua 1:8-9)

That was the hallmark of all the Old Testament believers we have been reading about.

May it be the hallmark of your life too.

About The Author

Val Waldeck, a well-known South African author, international Bible teacher and conference speaker, has written several books and writes regular columns for JOY, the South African National Christian magazine.

Email: val@valwaldeck.com

Website: www.valwaldeck.com

NOTE FROM THE AUTHOR: *Thank you for reading my book. If you enjoyed it, please take a moment to leave a review.*

Thank you!

More Books by Val

Bible Reading Plans

Biblical & Doctrinal Topics

Counseling

Devotional Christian Books

End Times

Entrepreneurs

Inspirational

Publishing

Religious Philosophy / Cults & Isms

See more publications on her website or on Amazon.

Subscribe to my newsletteron my website and receive this encouraging Ebook for free.

When the Storms Come is a powerful spiritual guide to overcoming and healing emotional, physical, and professional crises.

PROMISES
TO
CHERISH

A 7-DAY DEVOTIONAL

VIDA LI SIK

PROMISES TO CHERISH

Cover Art: Francine Beaton

Cover Photo: SunshineSeeds @ Depositphotos.com

Africa Icon: ©Shirley Corder

Acknowledgements

Thank you to Francine Beaton for creating the beautiful cover art on this book, but mostly, for your friendship and encouragement. It means the world to me.

Thank you also to my friends – Karen Suchecki, Keri Aguirre, Marc Jarchow and Sylvia Markey – for your friendship and help in polishing my writing. You are stars!

To our loving and

ever-faithful Father

who keeps all His promises

Contents

Introduction

I love rainbows. It's not because of the beautiful colours, amazing as they are. No, the reason why I adore them is because they symbolise a promise. In the book of Genesis, God promised mankind after the flood that He would never again destroy the earth with water. And He placed the rainbow in the sky as a visible sign of that promise. As someone who loves visuals, I can only say, "Wow!"

A promise is a declaration that someone will do exactly as they say or a pledge that something will come to pass. A promise gives you hope. It helps you forge ahead when your strength is low. It offers comfort when your spirit is crushed.

The Bible is full of promises that God made to His people. Most of them are implied rather than stated explicitly. We read in 1 Corinthians 1:20, "For no matter how many promises God has made, they are 'Yes' in Christ. And so through him the 'Amen' is spoken by us to the glory of God."

In this small booklet, I focus on a few of God's promises that mean a lot to me. Having lived in three and visited seven countries on the African continent, I've clung to God's promises when dealing with life's challenges. It is my hope that you will identify promises in the Bible that mean a lot to you. And that you will memorise and cherish them every single day.

Day 1

Finding God

"Then you will call on me and come and pray to me, and I will listen to you. You will seek me and find me when you seek me with all your heart."
(Jeremiah 29:12–13)

Most people usually focus on the verse just before this one – where God tells His people that He has plans for their lives.

But, the two verses above highlight that some effort is required from all of us. We can only find God when we seek Him with all our hearts. In Acts 17, the Bible tells us that God is not far from each one of us and that He has determined the exact times and places where we should live to make it easy for us to find Him.

People say that living in Africa is not for the fainthearted. And, when you look at the economic and political challenges that people face across the continent, you realise that it is not an idle observation – you do require a fair amount of resilience to thrive.

I lived in the Ivory Coast (in West Africa) for four-and-a-half years. Even before we got there we needed to get at least seven vaccines – hepatitis, tetanus, meningitis amongst others – because illness is very common in that part of the continent. In fact, the locals get malaria often and treat it as if it is the common flu. Hardships like poverty, illness and crime make it easier for the people on the African continent to recognise their need for God. The needs can be overwhelming, much more than for someone living in a first-world country. Praying and turning to God is so much easier to do when you experience hardship and suffering, and have nowhere else to turn but to God.

But, where does one find our Maker when He is not physically visible? You have to look for signs of Him. I see Him in a friendly smile, in the kindness from a stranger, but above all in nature. The sweet song of a bird, the intricate design of a flower or insect, the majestic mountains that rise towards the sky, the trees that extend their branches in praise to Him. And in God's Word.

From the first page of Genesis to the last one in Revelation, God pours out His love for us. And with the help of technology, in the form of the cell phone, it has never been easier to read His Word and to find God among the pages.

God is without limits, and always ready to listen to us, whether you whisper a prayer in the dark of the night, crying silent tears of anguish that soak into your pillow, or shout it from the rooftops. And, help is always at hand if you need someone to guide you to find God.

Reflection

How would you rate your efforts to find God? What can you do differently?

Thank You, Father, for the promise that we can find You if we seek You with all our hearts. It is comforting to know that You are only a short prayer away.

Day 2
Never Will I Leave You

"Keep your life free from love of money, and be content with what you have, for he has said, "I will never will I leave you; never will I forsake you."

(Hebrews 13:5)

God first made this promise to the Israelites in Deuteronomy 31:6 as they were about to enter the Promised Land. With a lot of uncertainty ahead and no clear indications on how to meet their need for food, clothing or shelter, this promise was important. How reassuring that God, who created heaven and earth, would go with them on their journey. They had a river to cross and many battles to win before they could sit back and relax.

I grew up in a family where I am the third-youngest and had 10 siblings. With so many mouths to feed and bodies to clothe, I received new clothes once a year at Christmas and had to be content with hand-me-downs the rest of the time. Yet, even though my family was not rich, I ate three meals a day. I did not have fancy toys and my siblings and I had to learn to be creative. We often made our own playthings – from kites made with bamboo shoots, newspaper and plastic, to "footballs" made from plastic grocery bags stuffed with newspaper and tied with string or sellotape.

Living in the City of Gold – Johannesburg – I felt God's protection on a few occasions when I was the victim of crimes and lived to tell the tale. Driving is also a challenge as I navigate the streets packed with aggressive drivers.

Today, as we journey through life, we learn how to be self-sufficient – get that job, the house, the car and a wife or husband. All these must-haves cost money. Even the wife or husband. In Africa, there are many inequalities and huge gaps between the rich and poor. Contentment can be hard to find. There always seems to be one more thing to save or strive for.

Yet, the promise that God will never leave nor forsake us holds true for us today as much as it did for God's people on the verge of crossing the Jordan river.

The writer of the book of Hebrews reminds us in the verse above not to put our trust in what we have (e.g. money or possessions) or to look at what we don't have, but to keep on trusting God to meet our needs.

The future may look very uncertain, and fear or discouragement may surround you. But, how you feel does not mean that God has abandoned you. He says, "*Never will I leave you*".

That means He will be there through good and bad times, whether your wallet is full or empty; irrespective of a fully stocked fridge or meagre pantry.

Reflection

Where will you put your trust today? God made a promise to the Israelites and to His children through the ages – it still holds true today.

Father, You are the God of plenty who can be fully trusted. Thank You for always being there for me.

Day 3

A Room for Us

"My Father's house has many rooms; if that were not so, would I have told you that I am going there to prepare a place for you? And if I go and prepare a place for you, I will come back and take you to be with me that you also may be where I am."

(John 14:2-3)

Growing up, I shared a bedroom with three of my older sisters. I only got one of my own in my teens.

We had bunk beds and I had to use a ladder to get to mine. As you can imagine, we had little privacy. The four of us shared wardrobe space for our clothes and shoes. Sharing a room had some benefits. It meant a lot of late-night chats and impromptu "karaoke" nights with our hairbrushes as microphones. But, as can be expected, there were also plenty of opportunities for conflict.

I had to wait until I was a teenager to have my own room, so you can imagine how much having my own space means to me. I've often tried to imagine what my room in our Heavenly Father's house might look like. Usually, it is something sizable, with a view of a mountain, the bushveld and the sea. It's not much that I ask [chuckle].

I am currently living in a house with no central heating. This is very common for homes in Africa where, to be fair, we enjoy great weather and snow is a rarity in many places. But, as someone who always feels the cold, I know that warmth will be a must-have in my room. Space would be another. And a fridge. I once stayed in a guesthouse in the picturesque town of Clarens in the Free State province. The room was huge. It had underfloor heating, a fireplace, a big, soft bed and a couch under the window – perfect for curling up with a book. And, it had an en-suite bathroom, of course. This was one of the best venues I've ever stayed in.

How comforting to know that there is a room waiting for me in God's house. The scripture only says "*a place*" without going into specifics. As a woman I love details. So, until I get to see it, I can only imagine what it looks like. Because Jesus is busy preparing it, I'm sure it will exceed all my expectations.

In the scripture above, the first thing that Jesus calls us to do is to trust Him. We need to trust that God has our best interests at heart. The best part is that Jesus says He will come back and take us to be with Him. To be in the presence of Jesus and our Father will exceed our wildest dreams. When we are with our big brother, Jesus, it won't matter what kind of room we get... His presence will be the best feature. But, knowing that He does everything well, we will not be disappointed.

Reflection

What does the room that Jesus is preparing for you look like? How much do you long to see it?

286

Thank you Jesus for taking the time to prepare a place for us. We cannot wait for You to come back and take us to be with you.

Day 4

Peace that Transcends All Understanding

"Do not be anxious about anything, but in every situation, by prayer and petition, with thanksgiving, present your requests to God. And the peace of God, which transcends all understanding, will guard your hearts and your minds in Christ Jesus."

(Philippians 4:6–7)

Peace – so elusive, yet so desired. We long for it, some search for it, while others are willing to fight for it. That is a sobering thought, and a contradiction in terms. Let's face it, there are enough things in this world to make us anxious, and it is very easy to worry about our families, our health, finances or even the future.

According to the dictionary, the Hebrew word for peace, "shalom", is more than just a greeting. It encompasses a wide range of meaning – completeness, totality, success, fulfilment, wholeness, harmony, security and wellbeing.

Its fullness is found in God. He is the source and giver of peace.

The verse above offers prayer as the solution to worry, and the peace of God as a promise to guard our hearts and minds. God's peace is very different from what the world promises. It is not positive thinking; it's not a zen-like calmness or the absence of noise or even conflict. Nor is it a promise that all your burdens will magically disappear.

Rather, it is the conviction and assurance that, even in the midst of turmoil, God is in control. It is the firm belief that God loves and cares for you; that He will never abandon you no matter what happens. And that God will carry you through every circumstance, whether your situation improves or not. God's peace will protect you from listening to Satan's lies, and will help you to continue cultivating the godly qualities you need in your heart.

In Africa, turmoil is often not far away. It can come in the form of political upheaval and power grabs. During our stay in the Ivory Coast, we witnessed how a once peaceful and stable nation was rocked by two coup d'états. These military overthrows of the government had social and economic repercussions that lasted for years. The people on the continent are familiar with suffering, but our response to disaster is often devoid of a sense of peace.

During Jesus's time on earth, and especially in the hours leading up to his crucifixion, He demonstrated what it meant to have "*the peace of God*". He went about His normal business with calmness and harmony, knowing full well that He would be falsely accused, abandoned by His friends, beaten and hung on a cross.

For us to get the peace of God in our lives, we need to imitate our Saviour and turn to God in prayer and surrender every circumstance to Him. That is easier said than done, but God's Son showed us how to do it.

Reflection

What does having the peace of God mean to you?

 Father, help us embrace and surrender to You in every situation, so we can experience the life of peace You intend for us to live.

Day 5

He Gives Strength

"He gives strength to the weary and increases the power of the weak. Even youths grow tired and weary, and young men stumble and fall but those who hope in the Lord will renew their strength. They will soar on wings like eagles; they will run and not grow weary, they will walk and not be faint."

(Isaiah 40:29–31)

In the last year of our stay in the Ivory Coast, my husband and then three-year-old son contracted malaria during the same week. My husband spent half a day in hospital on a drip filled with essential medicine. Back home, I had a toddler burning up with fever but who refused to take medication without putting up a fierce struggle. On top of that, I had given birth to our second son a mere two weeks before and had a little baby to take care of as well. Talk about being weary and weak!

Even the strongest among us can grow tired and feel powerless when life throws yet another challenge our way. Have you noticed how challenges tend to come at you in relentless waves rather than evenly spaced-out events? Maybe your reality is feeling depleted as you take care of others. Or, you get knocked down and feel unable to get up after a crushing disappointment. But, when you've reached rock bottom, there is someone to turn to.

God does not get tired. He is strong and powerful. He is never too busy to listen or help. He does not need sleep or rest. He never gets overwhelmed. No problem is too big for Him to solve. He is our source of strength. His strength never runs out. You can tap into God's energy to tackle whatever challenge comes your way. He will help you rise above the obstacles in your path—like an eagle soaring high above—and see them in a different light. Or like a marathon runner, you'll find an extra reserve of strength to persevere and keep going. In the same way, we can replenish our faith, patience and perseverance by drawing closer to God and relying on Him to see us through. Our Heavenly Father does not want us to go through life overwhelmed and defeated. He wired us in such a way that we get tired when we rely on ourselves, a job or even a relationship. Very often, He puts us in a community – people in our lives to lean on, and to see that the solution to our problems lies right in front of us.

Reflection

What stops you from relying on God when faced with life's challenges? How will you change that?

Thank You, Father, that you are strong when we are weak. Nothing is impossible for You. Fill us with power. Supply us with what we lack so we can grow strong and face each challenge with hope and perseverance.

Day 6

All These Will be Given You

"But seek first his kingdom and his righteousness, and all these things will be given to you as well."

(Matthew 6:33)

"All these things will be given to you." Who does not like the sound of that? It is a sure and certain promise that leaves no doubt about the outcome. But, what are *"these things"*? In the paragraphs before this verse, Jesus addressed some of our mundane yet very essential needs – food (sustenance) and clothes (protection). These necessities are the reason why we get out of bed, and go to work to try and earn some money to take care of our families. For many of us, the pursuit of money – treasure – becomes an all-consuming quest that takes our focus away from God. When our eyes focus on what we don't have it is easy to give in to worry. And, we know from experience that worry takes away rather than adds to our lives.

During my childhood, my father worked in the big city of Johannesburg – 75km away from our home in a little town on the East Rand. He would come home every second week and his car would be stacked with provisions. We looked forward to his arrival and always had great expectations of not just receiving the bare necessities but also some special treats. My father knew what we needed and would buy food in bulk. As a child, I was less interested in the basic food stuff but rather treats like sweets, biscuits and fizzy drinks.

In Africa, it is very common that fathers work in cities or towns situated far from their homes so that they can provide for their families. Some of them are only able to return home once a year (usually around Christmas) with supplies for their families. But parents know not to return home empty-handed. They would provide not only foodstuff and presents, but also uniforms and stationery for the next year of school.

Jesus says that His Father knows what we need even before we ask Him in prayer (in Matthew 6:8). He wants our focus and energies to be on seeking first His kingdom. God is king in heaven and on earth. When we embrace our King's commands and make an effort to do what is right and obey and please Him with our lives, then He says, "*All these things will be given to you as well*". Meaning, He is already willing to give us what we need in addition to the benefits we reap from seeking first His kingdom. We need to have an eternal perspective, peace and contentment as we trust that God will take care of us here on earth. But we have to turn to Him first, and not as a last resort when our own efforts fail.

Reflection

What makes it hard for you to turn over total control to God?

Father, you are more than able and capable of supplying all our needs. Help us to surrender and trust You without reservation.

Day 7

No More Tears

"He will wipe every tear from their eyes. There will be no more death or mourning or crying or pain, for the old order of things has passed away."
(Revelation 21:4)

Tears are quite amazing. They allow us to express both joy and happiness, but also pain and sorrow. Often, it is fairly obvious and easy to work out the reason behind someone's tears. We have tears of laughter while enjoying a comedy show, or to express joy when we see someone we love. The antics of a little child can be quite comical too and can have adults wipe away an emotional tear.

In Africa, weddings and funerals are occasions of joy and sorrow. Communities join to celebrate with the happy couple. Likewise, family and friends gather at funerals to offer comfort and support to those who mourn.

Right now, we have very little to laugh about as Covid-19 wreaks havoc in our lives. We cry over the loss of a loved one. We weep when we see the suffering that mankind inflicts on one another. The wounds inflicted by someone close to you are devastating. We mourn the loss of a job, our freedom to move around and our changed way of life. Gosh! We can even cry over the impact of poor leadership in our society.

Maybe you (like me) want to give up on watching or reading the news because it drives you to tears. On other occasions, the hurt and pain you experience is too much to bear or share. You use a pillow to muffle your crying in the still of the night until you fall into exhausted sleep.

But our Creator wants to encourage us. He wants you to know that He is near. No matter what you are going through today or how bleak the situation may look. Even when it seems as if all hope is gone, or when you wonder, where is the love? This is not the last word. He is ready to listen when you cry. You can go to Him at any time to express your worry, pain or sorrow.

It may not always be obvious, but God is with us. He is carrying you when you don't have the strength to take one more step. He is there when you try one more time, in the middle of a bad situation, to create a different outcome.

God promises to come and live with us in a new Jerusalem. He will be on hand to wipe away every tear, there will be no more pain, mourning or death. With our Father next to us, there will be no reason for pain or sorrow. His Word says "*there will be no more death, or mourning or crying or pain*". What an amazing promise. I know that it is something I look forward to.

Reflection

What pain or sorrow do you need to bring before God today?

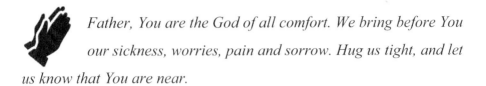 *Father, You are the God of all comfort. We bring before You our sickness, worries, pain and sorrow. Hug us tight, and let us know that You are near.*

Final Words

Thank you for taking this devotional journey with me. I hope it deepened your faith and love for the scriptures and that you enjoyed each devotional as much as I enjoyed writing them. We have not even begun to scratch the surface when it comes to finding God's promises in his word and embracing them in our lives. May you enjoy God's richest blessings in your personal walk with our Father.

About the Author

Vida Li Sik is a wife, mother, award-winning journalist and multi-genre author. She grew up in a small town, Nigel, in sunny South Africa, and developed a love for the scriptures as a teenager. She still takes every opportunity to deepen her knowledge of the Bible.

Together with her family, she is actively involved in a youth and family ministry in Johannesburg, the City of Gold. She has no pets and has yet to find a weird and wonderful hobby. In the meantime, she loves to write about people – real ones and imagined.

Find out more about books written by the author at her **website:** https://www.vidalisik.com/books

Contact her at: vidalisik@gmail.com

More Books by Vida Li Sik

Non-Fiction:

Devotionals for Women: 31 Days to Deeper Faith

Women's Fiction:

Aching Heart (Book 1 in the Heart Series)

Lonely Heart (Book 2 in the Heart Series)

Sports Romance:

Bowled Over

inspired to worship

through seven Psalms of David

Ann Goodfellow

INSPIRED TO WORSHIP

Acknowledgments

To all my family, friends, and those of the Body of Christ who have encouraged me to write for the Lord. Thank you!

To all those who have helped through proof-reading, editing, correcting grammar and content, publishing and printing, I am grateful for your support throughout this journey of writing.

Also to Shirley Corder and her team for all their support and helpful corrections and suggestions.

Thank You to our Lord and our God who gave me the desire to write for Him and has encouraged me each day as I have sat before Him with an open notebook and pen. He has inspired me and encouraged me day by day. To God be all Glory, now and forever more!

This book, as with all my writings, is dedicated to God Almighty, my Lord, my Teacher, and my Guide. He continues to inspire me each day to read His Word, to reflect on His message revealed, to write the thoughts He gives, and to make His lessons part of my living.

Table of Contents

Inspired to Worship is written in British English.

Introduction

I have always loved Psalms, because I have always loved poetry. Psalms stir me, and my emotions run deep as I read the expressive words. The words flow effortlessly, enlightening the message being brought.

Psalms bring deep meaning to the words being expressed. It is as though they are singing to the Lord, and in my mind's eye I can see David strumming his guitar—making beautiful music that will please the Lord.

During the next week of readings, I will be introducing you to seven psalms especially dear to my heart. As you read each psalm, imagine that David is in the room with you. See yourself watching and listening to him. Let the music and the words flow into your soul – and rejoice with David.

He wrote them from his heart-felt love for the God of all. As you read them let the message touch your heart and feel the love, adoration and praise that David expressed. Allow the words to resonate in your heart and use them as your own expression of love for the Lord. He rejoices over your desire to let Him know just how much He means to you. He is the Lord of all, high and lifted up, exalted and worshipped!

1

Happiness

"You are my portion, O LORD;
I have said that I would keep Your words.
I entreated Your favour with my whole heart;
Be merciful to me according to Your word.
I thought about my ways,
And turned my feet to Your testimonies.
I made haste, and did not delay
To keep Your commandments."
(Psalm 119: 57-60)

When are you happy? What makes you happy? Are you happy all the time despite setbacks, trials and difficulties?

Over 50 years ago I had to have a major kidney operation at a hospital in Johannesburg, and I can remember the other person in the ward asking me if I was scared of what I had to face. I answered, "No – not at all!" and that was the truth. There was no fear. I truly trusted that I would get through this. I faced the possibility of not surviving and was at peace. My faith and trust was in my Lord, and I knew that, no matter what happened, He was in control. He went before me into a difficult situation and ensured that all went well and my health was restored.

What is happiness? Is it a state of mind? Or being with someone you love? Or the fulfilment of a heart's desire? The one who fully trusts God Almighty finds that happiness is always with him. God's love enfolds him and enables him to face life with all its complexities, with joy. The happiness that comes from God sustains us in every way, so that even as we pass through troubles or loss there is within us a core of joy. That joy is a wonderful gift from God that sustains us through thick and thin. That joy comes from the relationship we have with God - Father, Son and Holy Spirit. It is built on faith, trust, love, and living fully in God's will. We are secure, knowing God's care, provision, and guidance for all of our lives.

It is seeking God, spending time in His presence, and taking note of His still, small voice. It is also obeying His prompting and knowing His touch and guidance in all your living. It is a relationship that completes you, and enables you to be the fullness of what God created you to be. Happiness is found through trust in God's grace, mercy and love!

In You, O Lord, I put my trust. You have never let me down. My hope and happiness is in Your hands as I live in whatever land You have placed me. I find joy where there is sunshine and a deep happiness that reaches deep inside me even during difficult times. The land where I live is also Your land, Lord. Help me to always remember that.

2

Who Do We Turn To?

"Hear my prayer, O LORD,

Give ear to my supplications!

In Your faithfulness answer me,

And in Your righteousness.

Teach me to do Your will,

For You are my God;

Your Spirit is good.

Lead me in the land of uprightness."

(Psalm 143: 1,10)

I have always been fiercely independent, wanting to make my own choices and decisions, but there came a time when I realised I needed help. There was an issue at work where someone was paying far too much attention to me, and no matter what I did to avoid the situation it persisted. What else could I do?

When we face trials and troubles to whom do we turn? When decisions have to be made and choices addressed, who can we speak to for advice? When we are sad and downcast from strife on all sides, where do we seek for help?

We might find help from family or friends, but the one who knows all about us is God, and it is to Him we must turn. He knows the sadness in our hearts, and that we need the comfort of a steadfast relationship, and He provides it. He knows the tears we shed in the middle of the night for our loved ones, and He gathers us close to assure us that He has them in His care.

He knows the way we berate ourselves over a wrong word spoken or a wrong deed done, and comes to tell us that we are forgiven and His love for us is still constant and true. God—Father, Son and Holy Spirit, is very near to comfort, console, support and strengthen those who turn to Him.

He stirs in our hearts and draws us near to hear His words of help and guidance. He reveals His will to us and as we step out to live as He wants us to we find a richness in our hour of need. He is always ready to hear the pleas of His children. We grow in our trust in our Lord as we see how He helps us in a difficult situation.

In the situation at work, His words of wisdom enabled the problem to be solved and I was able to go forward again with no fear of being harassed.

 We turn our faces towards You O Lord, pleading with you to guide us and help us in our daily lives. Guide and guard the leaders of our land, so that they do what You instruct them as they seek to keep Your people safe in a firm structure of government. May Your will be done in our lives O Lord!

3

The Lord Gives New Strength

"The LORD is my shepherd,

I shall not want.

He makes me lie down in green pastures;

He leads me beside the still waters.

He restores my soul;

He guides me in the paths of righteousness

for His name's sake.

Surely goodness and loving kindness will follow me all the days of my

life

and I will dwell in the house of the LORD forever."

(Psalm 23:1-3,6)

For an extended time in my life, I faced chronic illness. I always found comfort in reading this Psalm. God promises to always be near - to give new strength and guidance. His support and His peace gives me assurance. He helps me to face the day once more, trusting in His ability to give me strength to do all I have to do.

Time after time, God helped me through the problems of the day to a better tomorrow. My faith and trust in God and His ability grow stronger day by day as I place my problems into His hands and leave them for Him to deal with.

His presence with me continually helps me in the difficulties of my daily life. God knows just what is needed, and I trust that He will supply new strength to me as I seek to live as He desires.

His presence, goodness and loving kindness encourages me in my daily toil. I put my trust in our Almighty God, for He has promised to take care of me all the days of my life.

As He was with David, so He is with each of us, guiding, testing, encouraging and helping us every moment of our lives. We can give God thanks and praise for His loving, caring, compassionate attention to every detail of our lives.

Lord, we are facing difficult times across the world. Each country has its own set of problems, including crime, violence and corruption. Thank You that You take care of us each day. Our faith and trust is in You. Blessed Lord, guide and help us as we go about Your business of loving and caring for all people.

4

God With Us

"As the deer pants for streams of water,

so my soul pants for you, my God.

My soul thirsts for God, for the living God.

When can I go and meet with God?

My tears have been my food

day and night,

while people say to me all day long

'Where is your God?'"

(Psalm 42:1-3 NIV)

The wonder of my relationship with God is that He is always near.

One dark night, I called out to God, fearful and anxious over my health issue. I lay awake with my heart pounding, knowing that something was definitely wrong with my heart. I was anxious what the visit to the doctor next day would bring. God heard my cry and calmed me back to sleep.

As we cry out to Him, longing to hear His voice, He may bring to our mind some Bible verse that assures us of His love for us. Whenever we raise our hands to worship and our voices in songs of praise, the Holy Spirit stirs within us, leading us to pray. We may sense the closeness of our Lord.

Each day God is watching over us, taking care of us, and touching us with His infinite love. The deeper our relationship with God grows, the more intense our longing for His presence becomes. God is our all in all.

Praise God from whom all blessings flow. Praise God—Father, Son and Holy Spirit. God is with us!

I have seen how my longing for His presence is ever with me. I desire Him to come and gather me close to His side and speak to my heart of His loving kindness and compassion. I know God has been with me in every moment of my life, from my birth, through my difficult teenage years through to old age with its own challenges. So too for us all. His loving care is constant and true in all that He does for us, for He watches over His creation with brooding love.

As the deer pants for the water, so pants my soul for You, O God.

My soul thirsts for You, the living God. My heart belongs to You, O Lord. Fill me day by day with Your loving kindness, and make the desires of my heart aligned with Yours.

5

Turn to the Lord

"You will guide me with Your counsel,
And afterward receive me to glory.
Whom have I in heaven but You?
And there is none upon earth that I desire besides You.
My flesh and my heart fail,
But God is the strength of my heart and my portion forever."
(Psalm 73:24-26)

Many perplexing thoughts come into my mind when facing decisions that have to be made, wondering what to do and how to do it.

Some years ago, my husband, Ted, developed cancer, and he had to go for weeks of radiation therapy followed by daily tablets and other extensive treatment.

I remembered that God knew all things. He knew the confusion of my thoughts, my inability to make a clear decision because of all the "what ifs", and He brought clarity to my thinking. This was especially needed in dealing with the medication that had to be given to my husband.

I have found that as I come before God and set my thoughts on Him and not on my difficulties, He breaks through and brings peace to my troubled mind and shows me the way to solve my problems.

God brings peace. He is my strength, my understanding, and my decision maker. I need to rely on the Lord and not let circumstances confuse me. God is all knowledgeable. He guides and helps me every step of the way.

Each day I wake in His care, each night He watches over me while I sleep. He guides my footsteps every moment of my life. He is the One who places me where my talents can give Him glory.

In the five years that my husband suffered from the cancer and other debilitating conditions, I depended utterly on the Lord and prayed to Him. I needed His closeness, the comfort of His peace, and His loving support when I was struggling.

God rejoices when I seek to serve Him to the best of my ability. He helps me along life's pathway that leads to an everlasting life in His loving care.

When Ted's life came to an end, we as a family prayed for the Lord's touch upon us. Like a gentle cloud, He filled the car we were in, and we were able to face viewing the body of the man we all loved, with joy and not tears of despair.

We were sad, yes, but as we said goodbye to my husband—my life-long companion of over forty-eight years, and the father to my son and daughter, it was not with great, uncontrollable grief, but a gentle sorrow.

My faith and trust is in You, O Lord, and I depend upon You to take care of all the people of my land in the midst of the turmoil and troubles that have to be faced. You are my peace, Lord, and my faith and trust is in Your loving kindness and watchful care of Your own!

6

Faith and Trust in God

" Great is the LORD, and greatly to be praised

In the city of our God,

In His holy mountain.

We have thought, O God, on Your loving kindness,

In the midst of Your temple.

According to Your name, O God,

So is Your praise to the ends of the earth.

(Psalm 48: 1,9)

As I look at the world around us and all the trouble that there is, I wonder at the outcome of the violence and hatred that there is in man. I can only turn to God and ask for His hand to be upon all circumstances. He can stop all wars. He says, "Stop fighting, and know that I am God!" I pray that men and women will heed the call of the Lord and stop their war-mongering.

One evening, the husband of the lady who is my home help was killed by thugs as he stood at his front gate. He was just looking out at the road and the people passing by. Yet senseless people took his life.

God intended for all men to live in peace and harmony with each other, not to destroy others through their desire for power and control. I need to trust God in these difficult days. He is still in control of all of His creation.

I turn to God and seek His presence, and praise and thank Him for His grace and mercy in all circumstances. God is a God of love, kindness, caring and joy. In Him there is no unkindness, or hatred, or selfishness.

He has no evil qualities such as is evident in many men. As I seek the Lord, I ask Him to fill me with loving kindness, so that I can be in perfect harmony with all people. I try to listen to what God is saying to my heart and then respond with a promise to be faithful to Him in thought, word and deed. I long to give Him honour each day of my life. As He guides my footsteps, I give Him thanks for His loving kindness each day.

Lord, there seems to be fighting and ill-feeling amongst the people of every country in the world. In some places, people are scared to even stand at their front door because of the thugs who seek to kill and destroy. I pray for the safety of the citizens of my country, that they may turn to You and worship You in loving kindness and not seek self-gratification through bad behaviour.

7

Saving Grace of God

"He who dwells in the secret place of the Most High
Shall abide under the shadow of the Almighty.
I will say of the LORD, 'He is my refuge and my fortress;
My God, in Him I will trust.'"

"He will call upon Me, and I will answer him;
I will be with him in trouble;
I will deliver him and honour him.
With long life I will satisfy him."
(Psalm 91:1-2; 15-16 NIV)

All those who acknowledge God as 'Lord of All' have been given a wonderful promise. God says, "I will save those who love Me and will protect those who know Me as Lord!"

All who call on the name of the Lord will be saved. Though we may be in the depths of despair, or in major trouble, when we call out to the Lord, He promises to come to our aid.

Life is not easy and there are many instances when we want to run away from the position we find ourselves in. We need to turn once more to the Lord and know that He hears our cry for help. He will come to us as on angel wings.

I remember a time when I didn't feel well. I went to the doctor, only for him to say, "You have nothing wrong, you are just anxious."

I knew he was wrong in his diagnosis, so I went back to him a few days later for a further check up. He immediately sent me to hospital saying I had heart failure. After a pacemaker was fitted I was able to make a good recovery.

God had clearly gone before me into this situation, persuading me to insist on further checkups.

How good to remember that we are precious to the Lord. He will always respond to our call on His Name. He will protect those who love Him and seek His presence and His promise.

Let us give thanks to the Lord whose love for His own ensures total care and protection. Isn't it wonderful to know He watches over us with brooding love? His guiding hand is upon our lives and He will assure our safety and well-being all our days. He goes before us into each day and we can be certain that whatever comes our way, He will hold our hands and guide us through.

If we look to Him for protection and guidance for our lives, He will never disappoints us. His loving touch, and gentle words will always lead us.

Thanks be to our God, ever by our side, who encourages and guides us along life's pathways.

Thank You Lord for Your protection and guidance. Whenever we face situations that endanger us, remind us to turn to You! You know all things Lord, especially what is required when we face danger or trouble. Our faith and trust is in Your saving grace, O Lord. Thank You for Your watchful care of us all.

God is Love

Are you sure of your relationship with God? If you have not yet accepted Jesus Christ as your Lord and Saviour, you may want to do so right here and right now. By opening your heart to the Lord and praying this prayer, you can be assured that you are entering into a wonderful relationship with Him.

Lord Jesus, I confess that I have not been pure in thought, word or deed, and have lived far from You. Jesus, I do believe that You are the Son of God and that You died for my sin so that I might come before God Almighty and be acceptable to Him. I believe that God raised You, Jesus, from death and that You reign in heaven with Him. Just as I am, Jesus, I come to You, believing that You can make me a new person in and through the work of God the Father, Son and Holy Spirit. I confess You as Lord of my life. Amen.

As you commit to the Lord, He will come into your heart and forgive you for all that you have done that was not in accordance with His will. Turn from the past, repent of all your wrongdoing and walk forward into a new life in His care. You are His beloved child, and He wants to be in a relationship with you.

It is my prayer that as you have read and studied this book you will have drawn closer to God, and I rejoice if that is so. Yet the fullness of your relationship with God, your Father, is found only through acceptance of Jesus as your Lord and Savior.

The people of Israel will have nothing more to do with idols; I will answer their prayers and take care of them. Like an evergreen tree I will shelter them; I am the Source of all their blessings (Hosea 14:8 GNB).

About the Author

Ann Goodfellow lives in a retirement village in Gauteng, South Africa. She has been writing a Prayer and Devotional guide for over 35 years which is distributed to a wide community. She has been involved in many aspects of prayer, including teaching, intercession, and healing prayer.

Should you desire to receive the weekly Prayer Guide please contact the author at anngood@iafrica.com, and she will add you to the list.

Other Books by Ann Goodfellow:

Available directly from the author
or from Amazon.

God is Waiting to Meet You - *Building your relationship with God through daily prayer*

God wants us to be restored into a loving relationship with Him by accepting that Christ is His Son. God wants to walk with us each day, bringing love, peace and joy into all that we do.

God Wants You to Know Him - *A journey of discovery of who God is through daily prayer and reflection*

You may think that God is too high and holy to be bothered about you—wrong! God cares deeply about you and all of His creation. He created you in love, and He wants you to experience the depth of His love for you. He calls you to meet Him—God craves an intimate relationship with you.

God's Promises - *The lengths God will go to keep His promises*

There are multiple promises found in the Bible, and God always fulfils His promises. In fact, He will go to extraordinary lengths to do so. Because He loves you so much, He will never stop reaching out to you, and encouraging you to have faith and trust in His promises. As you take the risk of depending on God in your times of trial and trouble, He comes near and gives you the assurance of His abiding love and care – then He delivers you from the troubles you are facing.

God Wants to Bless You - *Discovering God's personal daily care for you*

Every day of your life is lived under God's richest blessings. He brought you into the world – He created you and is with you always. God wants to enrich your life by showering you with blessings that fall like gentle rain.

Today is No Ordinary Day - *Enjoying God's company in everyday life*

This book will help you to open your heart to the many ways God interacts with us – especially on our ordinary days. Find hope and a new perspective as you read and reflect. Your relationship with the One who guides and help you each day will be strengthened. He is our one constant companion. Allow Him to join you on the journey of life and show you that those ordinary days are special to Him. He wants them to be extraordinary for you because His loving care and help is with you every moment.

Encountering God - *A lifetime of a relationship with God*

This book was born out of an encounter with God, a fleeting moment when the author met with Him and felt His love and His grace in a very real way. That moment was so deep and moving that she desired to capture it in the written word and share it with others, so they – and you – can know the importance of encountering God.

Life on the Narrow Road - *Journeying with God towards eternity*

Your day by day life journey includes happiness and hardships as well as times of joy and difficulty. When life gets tough you can count on Someone who will never let you down. You don't have to travel through life alone - Jesus has been your constant Companion from before you were born, and will be with you long after you take your last breath. Listen to God - Father, Son and Holy Spirit – who often speaks to your heart and guides you to go this way or that, always helping you onward towards the gate that opens to eternal life – the narrow road that leads to Heaven.

The Path of the Pilgrim - *365 Guideposts along the way (also available in paperback through CUM Christian Books in South Africa.)*

The Path of the Pilgrim is a 52 week devotional that provides the seeker with guideposts along their journey with God. The reflections will enable you to find your way to Him, take His hand and go boldly into each day. As you seek the Light, you will find yourself loved, enriched and filled with assurance. Immerse yourself in the love of God, yield every day into His hands and take all that He wants to teach you deep into your heart.

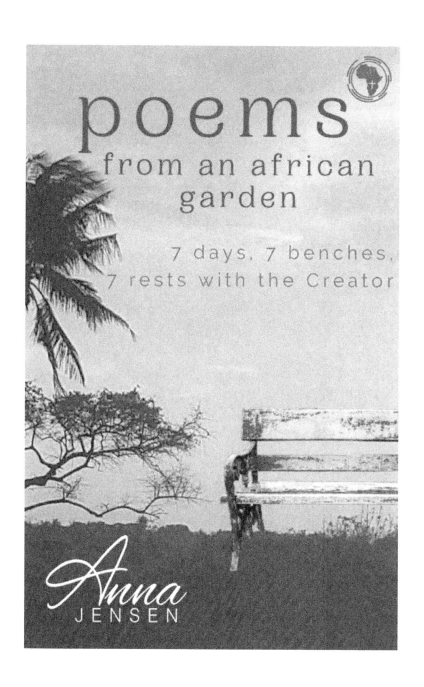

poems
from an african
garden

7 days, 7 benches,
7 rests with the Creator

Anna
JENSEN

POEMS FROM AN AFRICAN GARDEN

Acknowledgements

Thank you to **Craig**, **Caragh** and **Leal** for cheering me on my writing journey. You keep it real!

Thank you to **Alison Theron** for all your reading, editing and creative assistance. I look forward to a long partnership of book perfecting.

Thank you to **Gwethlyn Meyer** for being a friend who holds me to account and keeps the creative energy high.

Thank you to **Sheena Carnie** for your eagle-eyed perusal of my work. And for the lessons on style and writing conventions. You're much more approachable than a handbook!

*And thank you, **Jesus**, for releasing in me a whirlwind of words. May You take them wherever they need to blow.*

To the bench builders and poetry writers, creating places of reflection and rest in the gardens of our soul.

Contents

Benches of Rest

As you may have realised if you've read the devotions contained in 'Musings from an African Garden', I have been a garden lover since a young age when I enjoyed the delights of visiting the Sheffield Botanaic Gardens with my Nan (grandmother). We would spend hours together with my sister exploring and playing games of hide and seek.

You may also have read that though I love to visit gardens wherever I find myself in the world, I am not myself a great gardener. My delight comes from enjoying the efforts of others, absorbing the colours and scents which have been laid out in beautiful formality or wild abandon. Gardens minister to my heart and soul in ways other environments simply don't.

A friend of mine recently shared on Facebook a clip of a BBC programme that explored the role of social gardening, especially during the current Covid-19 pandemic and consequent 'stay-at-home' and isolation orders that have been imposed by governments around the world. This particular episode focused on a community in Northern Ireland where one man decided to remove the rubbish bins from a back alleyway between two rows of houses and in their place put some attractively planted pots and containers. Within a few days his neighbours became interested and started adding their own contributions. An ugly disused alley has become a place of recreation and joy. Gardens, even of the simplest variety, can transform lives.

There is one particular area in any garden to which I am always drawn — the garden bench. This can be situated in a wide open space or tucked away in a hidden nook, surrounded by expanses of manicured lawn or over-run by flowers and bushes. My reason for loving a bench? Because it provides a place of rest — not from the exertions of walking but from the exertions of life. Here I can sit and reflect, I can meditate and listen, I can be both quietened and envisioned.

In many ways a poem is like a garden bench; it offers a moment of pause and contemplation, an opportunity to think a little deeper and go beyond the simple. Within these pages I have offered seven 'benches' — seven poems of rest and reflection. Each pertains to an African garden I have visited and loved, and where I have seen a glimpse of our Creator God. The gardens are featured in my devotional 'Musings from an African Garden' which you'll also find in this box set. You may wish to read that first if you haven't already, although it is not necessary. I invite you to take a seat, take some time and invite Jesus to sit alongside while you enjoy His rest.

Just a short note about language before we continue our sojourn into the world of garden spaces. I am a most English author, despite having lived in South Africa for many years. I, therefore, use English expressions and spelling rather than American, so please forgive me if anything isn't clear to you or spelt as you might expect.

1

Solitude

'He brought me out into a spacious place;
he rescued me because he delighted in me.'
Psalm 18:19 NIV

I sometimes find life a little noisy, with much that shouts for my attention. There are family responsibilities, community concerns, global issues, all demanding that I take notice and respond appropriately. It can become so overwhelming that I find myself longing for silence — not the external quiet of an empty house or turned off television, but rather a deep silence of the soul.

In Psalm 73 Asaph writes of his anguish as he contemplates the 'prosperity of the wicked' and how they are 'always at ease'. He feels the vanity of his own pursuit of righteousness and is overwhelmed by the injustice he feels. Until, that is, he 'enters into the sanctuary of God'; here he is given perspective, he comprehends a bigger picture. He is brought into a spacious place where he can declare, 'But for me it is good to be near God; I have made the Lord GOD my refuge…'. He has found peace from the noise.

When I need that kind of peace — the silence that comes from entering the sanctuary of God — I slink off into my garden with a cup of strong black coffee and my Bible and simply sit. It is a wonderful thing to be drawn aside by Jesus…

Inhabited Solitude

Into this spacious moment of your caress
    you draw me
        cocoon me
           silence me.

Captured by a distant
              wide horizon
    held in everlasting arms underneath.
        Hedged
    Protected
        Boundaried
      Calm

As laying down the crown of me —
    the must do
      need to
        should have —
this racing treadmill heart
finally   pulses   slow.

    Inhale deep
Exhale full
      Breathe.

Withdrawn aside

     wooed

to abide in this inhabited solitude.

Jesus, thank you that You lead me beside quiet waters and You restore my soul. Help me to turn to You, my Good Shepherd, when the world around me has become noisy and overwhelming. Thank you that in Your presence I find perspective and understanding, enabling me to continue the journey in front of me.

2

Seasons

'For everything there is a season,
and a time for every matter under heaven.'
Ecclesiastes 3:1

Almost everyone I know in Durban loves aloes. During the summer months these ungainly succulents are nothing much to look at. In fact, it is easy to walk on past them without much of a second glance as they squat in tangled profusion in a flowerbed or alongside a road, hidden by the more attractive summer blooming plants. It is in winter that they shine, resplendent amid the dull browns and dusty greens of this, our rainless season. Stems grow and protrude from above their fleshy leaves, forming candelabras of bright colour — red, peach, yellow, orange and any combination of them all. Curve-beaked sunbirds are drawn to their nectar-filled stamens. Bees buzz in sweet delight. Drab, barren hills are alive with a flame-like blaze.

I find aloes are a yearly reminder to me that the timing of our Heavenly Father is perfect; He has seasons planned and prepared not just for plants, but also for us, His precious children. I may feel as though everyone around me is in full summer bloom while I remain hidden, unnoticed. I can so easily become frustrated or disappointed, even to the point of despair. Until I realise that another season is coming, a time appointed for me to blossom and flower.

How about you? Do you feel as though others are flourishing around you while you simply aren't? Be encouraged as you pause over this poem — His timing is always perfect, His ways are not ours, and He will bring you into a season of life and colour in a time that will delight and refresh all who see.

A note on this poem. Unlike most of my work which I write in free verse, 'Winter's Gift' is written with the strict rules of a sonnet applied. This may be an unfamiliar form for some, and therefore perhaps a little more challenging to read. But may I encourage you to take a little time and allow both the imagery and formality to speak gently to your heart.

Winter's Gift

Now summer's leaden blanket lies shredded
Extended shadows spread their creeping chill
Excoriated earth parched and weathered
Cloaked in misty pall, unheralded, still.

Branches once clothed in luscious feath'ry green
Now curl in withered spindly self-pity
Silent fragility, the new-crowned queen
Barren and stark her own kind of pretty.

Then studded across this landscape of brown
Jewels and gems are witnessed to flourish
Orange and red, the bright hues of sundown
The soul with their vibrancy to nourish.

This bare season's beauty, joy to the heart
Winter's sweet flow'ring the hope for restart.

Father, thank You that You have a plan and purpose for my life. Thank You that Your timing is always perfect. Help me to take my eyes off what You are doing with other people and instead seek You, so that I will be ready when You declare, 'Now is the time!'

3

Secure

'As I looked, thrones were placed, and the Ancient of Days took his seat;
his clothing was white as snow, and the hair of his head like pure wool;
his throne was fiery flames; its wheels were burning fire.'

Daniel 7:9

I don't know about you, but there are times when I wake up in the
morning and feel just as tired as when I went to bed the night before! It
isn't even that I've not slept well, I've just woken up not feeling
refreshed. Usually when this happens I realise I am overloaded and
overwhelmed, deafened by a world in crisis. I am desperately in need of
some peace, some quiet, and a different perspective. But where to find
them?

The Botanical Gardens in Harare, Zimbabwe, have some of the oldest
trees in the Southern Hemisphere growing there. These trees remained
strong, tall and solid throughout the tumultuous years of Rhodesia's fight
for independence and subsequent birth as the nation of Zimbabwe. They
have survived the noise of a country in turmoil. Their tops reach heights
that offer a perspective different to my own, earth-bound view.

Our God is described by Daniel as the 'Ancient of Days'. Jesus tells John in his vision on the island of Patmos that He is the 'First and the Last, the Alpha and the Omega' (Revelation 1:8). When I run into the tower that is the name of the Lord, I am saved (Proverbs 18:10); I am raised to a place of peace and security, a place where I can see more clearly.

Eternal

The overwhelming nature of this world's stage -

    every act an epic opera

        daunting script

      flamboyant costumes

Lights and sounds and action.

Tragedy, comedy,

    all writ large

An orchestral cacophony with deafening crescendo.

No interval in the programme.

Where to run?

    How to escape?

When will the curtain fall

    and silence descend?

Sneaking out to a wider space —

    a higher ceiling

        a vaulted, soaring majesty.

His ancients on display

    His Word the final say.

This moment from the escaped stage,

    absorbed in His eternal dance.

Swept along by outstretched arms
swirling in His delight
Seen, known, heard
Transformed.

Father, thank you that You are the same yesterday, today and tomorrow. Thank you that You are not changed by circumstances around You, but that You stand sure and strong, a safe place for me to run to and hide in. Help me to do that, especially when the noise of the world's stage becomes too loud.

4

Serenity

'The hearing ear and the seeing eye, the Lord has made them both.'
Proverbs 20:12

In Psalm 139 David states that we are fearfully and wonderfully made, knitted together perfectly by our Creator God. We have been given two eyes with which to see, two ears with which to hear, a nose, a mouth and a body alive with nerve-endings. Proverbs 20:12 highlights that the 'hearing ear and the seeing eye' are both made by the Lord. Our senses are part of our Godly make-up.

Our busy lives can so often lead to a sensory overload that prevents us from seeing clearly or hearing well. I forget to smell and carefully taste; my fingertips don't notice the feel of the surfaces they rest on.

Over the last few years the Holy Spirit has taught me the value and delight in deliberately and intentionally employing my senses, taking the time to notice, observe and mentally record my surroundings. As I do so, I also become more aware of the voice of the Holy Spirit Himself, perhaps reminding me of certain Bible verses or answering a concern that preoccupies my thoughts.

I have learnt to do this wherever I happen to find myself, but there are a few spots that are my especial favourites. The sunken garden in the Durban Botanical Gardens is one such place, a 'bench of rest' in my daily life.

Why not practice deliberately paying attention to your senses right now, wherever you are sitting and reading this. You might be surprised at what you discover!

May I

May I

    in awe

admire the architect's superior skill

      as the spider spins her web

and watch with fascinated interest

    the smallest ant

  with purpose

    scurry by.

May I

    with joy

attune my ear

      to the skylark's summer song

and listen with enrapt attention

    to the lilting of the shrike.

And may I

    with deliberate attention

  caress the rough-edged stone

and feel with gentlest of fingertips

    each tiny grain of soil.

May I

    inhaling deep

breathe the scent of Spring's first rain

the honeysuckle's perfume
　　　　and autumn's sad decay.

May I
　　with parted
　　　　thirsty
　　lips
taste the salt of ocean's spray
　　the sweetness of a new-cut meadow
　　　　the apple orchard's fruit.

May I
　　through Holy Spirit's whisper
seek to hone my inner sense
　to know when heaven's near
　　　to pause and pray
　　to sit, to wait
　　　　for this
　　　　Your Kingdom come.

Father, thank you that I am fearfully and wonderfully made by You. Thank you that this includes all my senses. Help me find a time and place where I can focus on using each of my senses, deliberately paying attention to what I can see, or hear, taste, smell and touch. Thank you that in doing so You will speak to my innermost being through Your Holy Spirit.

5

Suddenly

'And Hezekiah and all the people rejoiced because God had provided for the people, for the thing came about suddenly.'

2 Chronicles 29:36

I don't suppose many of us would connect the words 'tortoise' and 'suddenly', would we? But the tortoise that emerged out of the bushes next to the bench I was sitting on in the Kirstenbosch Gardens in Cape Town did exhibit a certain 'suddenliness', mainly because it was so unexpected. A rustling of leaves was all that presaged its appearance at my feet. Up until then, I had been quietly minding my own business, admiring the view.

Our lives with God can be a little like that. We may be sitting on a 'bench' not anticipating anything special, or be desperately seeking a breakthrough which doesn't come. But just like the rustle of the leaves beside me forewarned me that something was coming, God proclaims: 'Behold, the former things have come to pass, and new things I now declare; before they spring forth I tell you of them.' (Isaiah 42:9)

In the first year of Hezekiah's reign as king of Judah, he reopened the temple and instituted reforms that led to the restoration of the priesthood and a revival of worship amongst God's people. There was great rejoicing at this sudden turn of events after the years of rebellion that had gone before.

God delights in 'suddenlies' — moments where He provides miraculously for us, His precious children. Sometimes all we can do is to sit and wait patiently.

Suddenlies

Shepherds resting with their flocks at night
    suddenly bathed in angel's light
The unexpected hallelujah
    of a birth-announcing chorus.

Far from home, in desert land
    Moses stood with staff in hand
Arrested by a bush aflame
    a holy, burning rendezvous
        with the great I Am.

A rainbow in a weeping sky
    The Son of God in persecutor's way
A jail door opened
    A wall in ruins
        A nation's faith restored.

Heaven's bursting brilliance on an unsuspecting earth.

Yet, sitting here in silent contemplation —
    or in frustrated stagnation —
do I believe His suddenlies
        are for me?
Lingering a little while
    pausing for a moment

perhaps I hear a rustling leaf

or watch a springing forth —

eager proclamation of Your anticipated Kingdom.

Thank you, Lord, that You are the God of 'suddenlies', bringing about change when I am perhaps least expecting it. Help me to be attentive to the rustle of the leaves, to the new thing that You announce before it comes to pass. And help me when I become impatient or discouraged. Thank you that Your timing is always perfect.

6

Selection

'...that you, being rooted and grounded in love....'
Ephesians 3:17

When I first moved to South Africa from the UK a little over twenty years ago, I felt I was embarking on a grand adventure. I was newly married, moving to a country on the other side of the world from where I had grown up, about to experience the wild and the wonderful. It only took a few months for reality to sink in, and for me to realise that I wasn't on holiday but actually needed to learn how to get on with this new life.

The breakthrough came when I read the parable of the two eagles and the vine in Ezekiel 17. I felt the conviction of the Holy Spirit that I had been transplanted from my home country to South Africa for a divine reason, and that, provided I remained 'rooted and grounded in [His] love' I would flourish and thrive in my new location.

This was confirmed to me when I visited the Eden Project on a holiday visit to my parents in England. Here were plants that belonged back in South Africa and yet were growing in a disused quarry in Cornwall. They were nurtured and protected under the cover of the innovative biomes that had been designed and built for just that purpose.

If horticulturists and architects took this much care of flora, how much more would my Heavenly Father care for me?

Do you sometimes feel planted in the wrong place, or as though your roots are withering where they are? Be refreshed and watered in the love of God for you, His precious child.

A note on the poem. This is a 'shaped' poem, whereby the layout of the words says as much as the words themselves. In this case, Part I represents the tree above ground and Part II the roots below. Allow the words and the shape to minister to you as you read them prayerfully.

Being Rooted

Being rooted –
  The visible and unseen.

Part I

Dancing leaves
Bending bows   swaying with the storms
Scented petal blossoms

Tissue paper

delicate

Nectar;

Life and promise

Fruitful and harvest

Abundance

and

a

refuge.

Part II

Tangled

fibres

reaching, seeking

gossamer fingers   probing

Capillaries   embedded   deep

draw   from subterranean   artesian   wells

of   eternal   overflow

Resolute

Secure

Established

In this

Your infinite

love

Father, thank You that I am rooted and grounded in Your love, knowing that I will be watered and nurtured regardless of where I am planted. Help me to spend time in Your presence when I feel dry and thirsty, drawing from Your water of life.

7

Surrendered

'His master said to him, "Well done, good and faithful servant. You have been faithful over a little; I will set you over much. Enter into the joy of your master."'
Matthew 25:23

When we visited our friend British at his home in Swaziland, we made much of his garden — not because of its beauty or pretty flowers, but because it was well worked. Large cabbages and tall cornstalks grew in carefully dug and weeded furrows of rich brown soil; chickens pecked the ground. British and his family exhibited pride and satisfaction in the result of their labour.

What better end to our own lives here on earth than that Jesus would welcome us into eternity with the words, 'Well done, good and faithful servant. Enter into the joy of your master.' (Matthew 25:23)

I am placed on this earth for a purpose; I am saved by Jesus and there are good works planned in advance for me to carry out (Ephesians 2:10). May I not always seek a soft armchair of ease when I am called to a bench of momentary pause from earnest toil!

No Ordinary Garden

Purchased at the highest price
        chosen —
                with intricate care
Sheltered from the harshest wind
        protected from the storms.

Hard ground broken
        ploughed and furrowed
                softened by a gently falling rain
        warmed, caressed and kissed
                by sunshine's rays.

Seeds selected with attentive gardener's skill
        understanding what will grow
                and blossom where it's sown.

Delicately placed —
        with deliberate intention
covered by the nurt'ring loam of love.

Seasons come —
summer's glare
        autumn's amber palette.
winter's hibernating grip.

Whilst far beneath
> away from sight and all disturbance
a germinating destiny explodes.
> Extra-ordinary miracle
> > and a purposed transformation.

Spring arrives —
> and with it, promise of the future
emerging bright and sweet and strong
Foretaste of what fruit will hang
> in this,
> > no ordinary garden.

Father, thank you that You are an energetic, creative God who has work for me to do too. Help me to find those things which You have planned in advance for me, and then to apply myself diligently to do them. My heart's desire is to hear You say, 'Well done, good and faithful servant.'

About the Author

I'm a British ex-pat who has lived in South Africa for a little over twenty years. My husband and I live with our two teenage children on the east coast, a few miles north of the city of Durban. Our garden overlooks the Indian Ocean where we have the privilege of watching dolphins and whales at play.

My first book 'The Outskirts of His Glory' was published in May 2019. The book is a Christian devotional and poetry collection exploring the many, surprising ways that God can speak to us through His creation. I have drawn on my travels in and around South Africa, as well as further afield, to hopefully inspire each of us to slow down and perhaps listen more carefully to the 'whispers of His ways' (Job 26:14) that are all around us.

Since publishing 'Outskirts', I have had the privilege of speaking at a number of local churches and even have a weekly slot on a Christian radio station. I have also continued writing by contributing to a variety of blogs and online writing communities as well as developing my own website and blog.

Want to know more? You can find me at

Website: www.annajensen.co.uk

I send out a more-or-less monthly newsletter which you can subscribe to on my website if you'd like to find out what's happening in the world of Anna! It includes my latest blog post about whatever God is saying and doing in my life at any given moment; there are also book reviews, guest posts and promos. It's free and you can unsubscribe whenever you like.

Email: I'd love to hear from you too. You can email me at hello@annajensen.co.za

More from Anna

If you enjoyed this devotional from Anna, you might like to check out her other books. You can find them on Amazon sales pages, or you can buy direct from Anna's website www.annajensen.co.uk

The Outskirts of His Glory

Join Anna Jensen and her family as they travel to seek out and experience the odd and unexpected of God's creation.

Captivated by the Creator (paperback only)
Be inspired afresh by the voice of the Creator through the beauty of His creation. Be guided by Anna Jensen as she describes her own journey of discovery through articles and poems. This beautiful journal contains pictures for you to colour and space for your own thoughts and prayers.

Twenty Years an Expat

Read about Anna's experiences as she leaves her native land and learns to embrace the different and the new as she settled in South Africa. At times funny, at others poignant, the one constant is God's love and purpose for Anna in all she experiences.

Poetry and Prayer

Anna started writing poems in earnest just a few years ago...Her poetry will always begin and end with Jesus. He is the master craftsman, the great author, The Word. In this way, each poem is indeed a prayer — of thanksgiving, of worship, of truth — whispered in her innermost parts. As you read both the poems, and the thinking behind them, it is her prayer that Jesus would woo you afresh with His presence.

Musings from an African garden

Take a moment to muse with Anna Jensen in seven of her favourite African gardens. Discover with her the delights of quiet contemplation, finding glimpses of the Creator God in every leaf and flower.

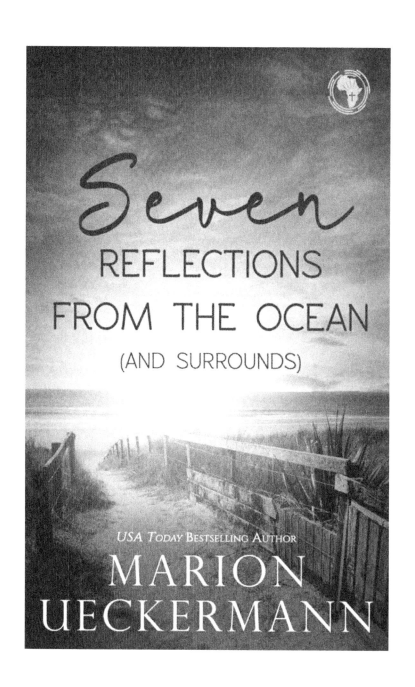

Seven

REFLECTIONS
FROM THE OCEAN
(AND SURROUNDS)

USA TODAY BESTSELLING AUTHOR

MARION
UECKERMANN

SEVEN REFLECTIONS FROM THE OCEAN
(AND SURROUNDS)

Seven Reflections from the Ocean
(and Surrounds)

The week of devotions in *Seven Reflections from the Ocean (and Surrounds)* was inspired by the coastline of South Africa. Each starts with a relevant scripture verse and ends with a heartfelt prayer.

From the author's childhood memories to present day troubles, readers will be encouraged not to fear the rough seas or the winds. They'll be challenged to make a difference, right where they are placed, and leave a legacy that lasts. Most important of all, they'll be reminded of just how precious and oh so loved they are by their Heavenly Father whom they can trust implicitly, even when it seems that He's not there.

Praise for Seven Reflections from the Ocean (and Surrounds)

This book is filled with tender memories, deep reflections, soul-searching questions, and heartfelt prayers. Each reflection is introduced with excellent and appropriate Scriptures that really enhance each section. It was a pure joy to read, and I know it will bring peace and hope to any heart. Besides reading it personally, I would highly recommend this book as a wonderful gift to give. It is a book that will beg to be both read and shared more than once.

~Becky Smith

The varying moods of both the ocean and life are beautifully reflected in these devotions with the stabilising factor of our one true anchor. What a blessing!

~ Ailsa Williams, Editor

I loved these devotions set on beaches in South Africa. I live twelve miles from the beach that's closest to me on the Atlantic ocean here on the Space Coast of Florida. As soon as I read these, I could see my own beach and remember times like these. I've never found sea urchins on the beach, but I've picked up my share of shells. Every time I'm at the beach, I think of how powerful the waves are, and know that God is even stronger, and yet He's there and He loves me, and He cares for me. As I read these devotions, it was like Marion wrote them just for me.

~ Trudy Cordle

When you can't visit the ocean, Marion Ueckermann brings the calming effect of water, sand, and air to you in seven reflections, plus scripture, prayers and photos. Meditate on God's immense paradise of South Africa, Cape Town, Table Mountain, Blouberg Strand, and the Atlantic Ocean. Unwind from your cares, escape your environment and relax with God's presence by the ocean with sand, pebbles, wind and more. No passport or plane travel required.

~ Renate Pennington, Retired English, Journalism, Creative Writing High School Teacher

Seven masterpiece reflections gracing pages straight from the heart. A glimpse of God's grace and love He shares with us each minute of the day. Pondering thoughts with true meaning that will capture your soul.

~ Sharon Dean

Seven Reflections from the Ocean (and Surrounds) by Marion Ueckermann is a collection of sea themed devotions that really focus the mind on the awesomeness of our God.

God is in charge of the macrocosm of the universe and the microcosm of you and me. As we journey through life, we can see His footprints in our lives. He guides us through storms. He is our anchor and He leads us through the fog. Marion Ueckermann has produced seven powerful devotions that will speak into our lives.

~ Julia Wilson, Book Reviewer at Christian Bookaholic

The devotions contained in *Seven Reflections From The Ocean (and Surrounds)*, written by Marion Ueckermann, warmed my heart and gladdened my spirit. Yes, they are indeed beautifully written, but even more, pondering the message in each one comforted and inspired. I will read these nuggets of truth again and again.

~ Jan Elder, Author of the Moose Creek Series

371

Marion can really make a book come to life. It's as if you can feel the sand on your feet and see the little one running with the biggest smile upon his face. And to know that God knew on this day that he would calm the seas for this family before they were ever even born… Such an amazing story.

~ Sherry Ferguson

The South African beaches are a wonderful setting for these devotions. *Seven Reflections from the Ocean (and Surrounds)* made me feel just like I was walking on the beach and feeling the salt water and wind blowing on my face. Seeing the beauty that God has created for us and feeling its calming effect is just amazing. I love how Marion brought in the story that was in the Bible of Jesus and His disciples on their fishing trip, and also how she personalized the story by the telling of their own trip to the ocean. When going through life, some of our plans get changed for reasons unbeknownst to us, but it is not for us to question God but to put our faith in Him because he always has our best interests at heart.

~ Terry Silva

Marion Ueckermann lives in beautiful South Africa. She takes everyday beauty and reminds us of the great wonders of the LORD. In the simple pebbles on the beach to the mighty winds, Marion helps us see beauty and God's love for us in the everyday. His handiwork is everywhere if we will only take time to look. These devotions are uplifting and the prayers are blessings we all need to pray for. Thank you, Ms. Ueckermann, for these reminders of His glory.

~ Renette Stee

Contents

For the One who created the oceans...

Jesus

If I go up to the heavens, you are there;
if I make my bed in the depths, you are there.
If I rise on the wings of the dawn,
if I settle on the far side of the sea,
even there your hand will guide me,
your right hand will hold me fast.

~ Psalm 139:8-10 (NIV)

1

Reflections in the Wind

"He let loose the east wind from the heavens and by his power made the south wind blow."

(Psalm 78:26)

There's just no escaping it… Cape Town is windy. Especially from September to March—or spring to late summer—when the strong, persistent winds blow, battering the Western Cape shores. On some of these blustery days, Capetonians can be found struggling to stay on their feet, clutching onto street poles and walls, or chasing after garden furniture—been there, done that last one at my son's house when the stiff breeze blew the trampoline clear across the garden. Thankfully, the boundary wall stopped it from traveling farther.

The locals call this yearly Cape phenomenon the South-Easter.

I remember when we visited the Cape one November almost three decades ago. We were swimming in a tidal pool with our sons, then aged three and five-and-a-half. My oldest was paddling about on a small, inflatable pool mattress when a gust of wind suddenly cropped up and began blowing him out toward the ocean. My husband sprang into action, and with the prowess of an Olympic swimmer, swiftly rescued our child from sure disaster.

"It's an ill wind that blows no good" is a popular English idiom that reminds me very much of the winds in Cape Town. I always saw this phrase in a negative context, but actually, the idea behind this saying is that even when bad things happen, there must be some positive results.

Now the South-Easter is affectionately known by another name—the Cape Doctor. This is because there's a belief that the continual winds clear Cape Town of pollution and pestilence. After a visit from the Doc, the city is clean and healthy, sporting clear blue skies. In my book, that's definitely a huge positive.

Yet another positive is that a thick mist forms over Table Mountain when the South-Easter blows up its steep slopes and meets the colder air at the top. Locally, this vaporous cloud that pours over the sides of the iconic flat-topped mountain on otherwise cloudless days is called the tablecloth. This spectacular covering makes it look as if the table is set by God himself.

Cape Town's winds are also perfect for the popular sport of kitesurfing—of course, not the 160km* per hour ones. There's nothing I love more than sitting on Blouberg beach on a breezy day, watching the myriad of colorful kites as paragliders skim across the ocean and over waves before leaping high into the sky.

But all's not fun and games in this beautiful part of the world. The hundreds of shipwrecks along the Cape Peninsula bear witness to why this South African coastline is rightly known as the Cape of Storms.

What about you? How do you perceive the ill winds that blow through your life? Are they like the Cape of Storms that threaten to dash you against the rocks and leave you shipwrecked, a broken vessel unfit to sail again? Or do you, like the Apostle Paul, see these tempests as light and momentary troubles that are achieving an eternal glory? Are you using your prevailing winds or storms to blow away and remove the things that weigh you down? They can change you for the better—you just need to trust in the One who rides on the wings of the wind and makes the clouds His chariot.

* 160km per hour = 100 miles per hour

"Jesus, when the winds come, as they will, please help me to stand firm. Remind me often that after the rain, there will always be blue skies. Help me weather whatever life throws at me, and to use the storms to shape me into the person You want me to be. Amen."

2

Reflections in Pebbles

"Then he took his staff in his hand, chose five smooth stones from the stream, put them in the pouch of his shepherd's bag and, with his sling in his hand, approached the Philistine."

(1 Samuel 17:40)

Many years ago, I helped my eldest son move to Cape Town (for the second time). Between unpacking boxes and buying missing items for his new home, we managed to find some time to spend together on the beach. It was wonderful and just the break we needed.

We walked across the soft, white sands of Bloubergstrand, Table Mountain a faded blue in the distant background, until we reached the darker wet sand of the ocean's boundary. As we strolled along the shoreline, we searched for shells, kicking and poking at seaweed that had washed ashore.

But the ocean hadn't washed up shells on this pristine beach. Rather, pebbles dotted the tidemark. Every now and then, I would stoop to pick up one that had caught my eye. Soon I held a handful of shiny, smooth pebbles which I slipped into my pocket.

A few months later, I sat on a different beach, in a different part of my homeland, South Africa. My husband and I were holidaying at Umhlanga on the KwaZulu-Natal coast. Now the beaches on the eastern side of South Africa are vastly different, the coarse granulated sand with its varying shades of tan a stark contrast to the soft, white sand of the Western Cape.

Again I found myself walking a sun-kissed beach, stepping over shells left by retreating waves where wet greeted dry. Finally, we chose a less inhabited area on which to relax, and watched the ebb and flow of the ocean as we soaked up the remaining afternoon sun.

As I sat gazing across the ocean, I suddenly realized that the small section of beach we sat on was different. Pebbles, large and small, lay scattered in the sand, revealed with every ebbing wave.

Nearby, a child chattered wildly, drawing my attention. I glanced across to see a small boy, around three years of age, having fun with his dad as they threw stones into shallow rock pools.

"Splash," he squealed with delight.

"Splash," his father echoed, relishing the time with his son.

Splash, and my thoughts turned to the ripples that falling pebbles create as they connect with water.

Fifty-four years ago, Senator Robert F. Kennedy delivered his "Ripple of Hope" speech at the University of Cape Town during a visit to South Africa. This was at the height of apartheid, and many believe this address was the greatest speech he ever made.

"It is from numberless diverse acts of courage and belief that human history is shaped. Each time a man stands up for an ideal, or acts to improve the lot of others, or strikes out against injustice, he sends forth a tiny ripple of hope, and crossing each other from a million different centers of energy and daring those ripples build a current which can sweep down the mightiest walls of oppression and resistance."

When David slew Goliath, he picked up five smooth stones and put them in the pocket of his shepherd's bag. Five...yet it took only one small stone to bring down the Philistine giant.

God has chosen you to be His pebble in the sea of humanity. What ripples of hope could emit from the splashes of your life? What giants could tumble from the impact of one small stone, one random act of kindness?

"Lord, I'm available. Use my life to change the lives of others. Help me to be the Good Samaritan, the one who speaks for those who have no voice, the one who washes feet. May what I do today create a positive ripple effect into eternity. Amen."

3

Reflections on Rough Seas

"We have this hope as an anchor for the soul, firm and secure."
(Hebrews 6:19)

During the coronavirus lockdown in South Africa, I found myself stuck in Cape Town with my son and his family. I'd come for a wedding in March and planned to stay to watch the grandkids during their school holidays, my ticket home booked for April 2nd.

Well, that didn't happen. The lockdown that brought our country to a standstill at the end of March ensured that I couldn't return home. The travel bans imposed kept me in the Mother City. Besides, I was needed to look after my grandchildren when my son and his wife returned to work but schools remained closed.

One morning, while homeschooling my eldest grandson, he had to answer a bunch of riddles as part of his English lesson. It boggled my mind that ten-year-olds were expected to figure out these riddles because my son and I only knew one each. Of course, Google came to the rescue.

One of the riddles read: "When you need me, you throw me away. But when you're done with me, you bring me back."

In hindsight, the answer seemed so simple: an anchor.

We all know that an anchor is a heavy metal device used to connect a vessel to the bed of a body of water. Wind and currents can cause a boat or ship to drift, but not when the anchor has been dropped.

People can be anchors, too. You know, that person who can be relied on to keep something in the right place, whether it be a project, a company, or a family, because anchors provide stability.

But there *are* times when it's not wise for a ship to drop anchor too soon. In a raging storm, the best course of action is for that vessel to find a safe harbor, one protected from the wind and the sea, and only then to drop anchor.

Years ago, my husband and I took a holiday in Umhlanga, just north of Durban on South Africa's east coast. As we enjoyed breakfast on the patio of our third-story holiday apartment one morning, we gazed out at the glistening ocean. Slowly, the sky darkened as ominous clouds encroached on the coastline. White-topped waves began to ripple the undulating seas, a telltale sign that the ocean's calm belonged to yesterday.

Life can be like that—one moment calm, the next tumultuous.

As I watched the ships on the horizon, seemingly unmoving, firmly anchored to the ocean floor, I was reminded that how we get through the turbulent moments of life depends entirely on where our anchor lies.

You and I will face many tempests as we sail the seas of life. These can come in the form of financial problems, job losses, illness, divorce, or the death of a loved one. When you're tossed about and fear you may drown, never forget that God is your anchor. His strong arms are the safe harbor in which to hunker down until the storm has passed.

If you're sailing rough seas, let me encourage you to anchor yourself in Jesus. And you do that by staying firmly grounded in His Word. Yes, your sails might get a little torn, your ship left battered after the gale, but take courage…you'll be able to weather the mighty gusts because of the One who gives peace and provides stability no matter how high the swells or crashing waves.

Isaiah 26 verse 3 promises, "You will keep him in perfect peace, whose mind is stayed on You, because he trusts in You."

Jesus remained serenely asleep in a boat in the midst of a terrible tempest. And because of Him, you can too.

 "Father God, how wonderful to know that You are the ONE Anchor that WILL hold, despite the storm. I'm trusting You to guide me through the rough seas of [sickness, divorce, unemployment, isolation, death]. Amen."

4

Reflections on the Beach

"Because of the Lord's great love we are not consumed, for his compassions never fail. They are new every morning; great is your faithfulness."

(Lamentations 3:22-23)

What is it that draws people to pick up shells when strolling along a beach? I have so many shells that I've collected from all over the world—from the white sands of Cape Town's beaches to the black shores of Raglan in New Zealand, and a myriad of places in-between. To be honest though, I could only tell you where one or two came from.

My latest additions are green sea urchin shells that my niece and I picked up on the beach in front of her seaside home on the west coast of South Africa. She'd been alone for several weeks, her husband stuck on the other side of the country due to the coronavirus lockdown. He'd gone on a business trip and couldn't get back home. I went for a few days to help her meet some work deadlines.

As we took her dogs for a walk on the empty beach late that first afternoon, we spotted the small, round, green shells. I've never seen these particular shells on a beach before. My niece shared with me that she rarely sees them, either, but during this period of isolation as she'd walked her dogs in the evenings, she had seen such a plethora of sea urchin shells.

"It was as if God was saying to me, 'I see you, and you are precious'," she said.

How incredible that God would use something as simple and small as a sea urchin to let one of His hurting children know she was not alone. To Him, she mattered more than words can say.

In my novel, *Remember Me*, which is the first book of the Chapel Cove Romances series, I came up with a line I absolutely love: *Collecting the shells the ocean offered up every night, were like God's mercies—new every morning.*

If you're feeling downhearted and tempted to think that you don't matter, take a walk along the beach with God, even if only in your mind, and let Him show you just how much He cares for you. When you start to count your blessings, it'll be like picking up shells on a shelly beach.

The prophet, Elijah, at the Lord's instruction, waited on the mountain for the Lord to pass by. A great and powerful wind ripped through the mountains, but God wasn't in the wind. Then came an earthquake. He wasn't in the earthquake. After that, a fire, but God wasn't in there either. He was in the gentle whisper that Elijah heard.

Too often we want God to speak to us in a big, noisy way. More often than not, He shows up in small, mundane things, like tiny sea urchins washed up on a deserted beach. Just. For. You.

 Abba Father, thank You that You see me, and You Love me.

Thank You that even when I'm lonely, I am never alone. Please remind me, Lord, when the billows of life knock me off my feet, to count my many, many blessings. Amen.

5

Reflections on the Ocean

"In their hearts humans plan their course, but the Lord establishes their steps."
(Proverbs 16:9)

In January last year, my husband and I took a four-day cruise from Durban up the coast of Mozambique with our son, his wife, and our two grandsons. Because there's a six-hour drive between Pretoria, where we live, and the coast, we drove down two days earlier to ensure we could meet our 11 a.m. boarding time. We spent the weekend at a beachfront holiday resort some ninety-minutes south of the port where we were to board midmorning on the Monday.

The day after we arrived at our apartment, we all took a walk down to the beach. This was the first time our five-year-old grandson saw the sea, or felt beach sand between his toes (except for when he was a year old, which didn't count in his or our books as he couldn't remember).

As he ran across the beach, he gathered up sand in his small hands and flung it into the air, shouting, "This is the best thing ever!"

The surprise birthday present for my husband of deep-sea fishing with my son at Pomene, one of our Mozambican stops, was also going to be the best thing ever.

Or so we thought.

Plans all began to change when the cruise ship got stuck at sea in Cape Town during one of those infamous Cape storms. We anxiously watched the news the weekend before our cruise as the ship remained anchored at sea overlooking Cape Town, unable to steer into the harbor due to the strong winds. Finally, it was safe enough for the vessel to enter, offload passengers and welcome new ones on board. Then the captain steered the ship at full throttle, even skipping the stop in Port Elizabeth in order to get to Durban on the other side of South Africa in time for the cruise north to Pomene.

The MSC Musica arrived a few hours later than it should have. Finally we were able to go through customs and board the gigantic liner with its sixteen decks. Two or three hours later than planned, the ship set sail.

But that wasn't the only change we'd encounter. Whilst at sea, we were informed that the route had changed and the additional day farther north to Pomene would no longer happen. Subsequently, the deep-sea fishing excursion was cancelled. The reason for the change, however, wasn't due to the delay in weighing anchor. A cyclone had pummeled the Mozambican coastline not long before and damaged the cruiseline's land facilities. So instead, the ship spent two days anchored off the same Portuguese island that we were meant to spend only one day visiting.

On the upside, all these storms happened before we set sail and not while we were at sea. I had watched one too many YouTube videos before our ocean holiday of cruise ships being tossed about on a tumultuous ocean to want to experience that for myself. I can only imagine how the disciples must've felt when caught in that terrible storm—the one Jesus slept through.

So whilst disappointed that the birthday present plans were spoiled, we were extremely grateful for smooth waters and calm blue seas.

Often we think that something is going to be the best thing ever, and it is. But there are times that it isn't. And when our plans change, we need to look at our situation in the light of God's omniscience because He's looking out for us, steering us to smoother, calmer waters.

I'll never know why my husband and son didn't take that fishing trip. But God knows, and for me, that's enough.

"Thank You, Jesus, that You have my back. Your eyes run to and fro throughout the earth to show Yourself strong. Your hand is not too short to save us. Your ears aren't deaf to our cries. You are always watching over us, always listening to our pleas, always reaching out to us. We don't deserve Your grace, but You give it anyway. You give us the best days ever. Thank You. Amen."

6

Reflections in the Sand

"Even to your old age and gray hairs I am he, I am he who will sustain you. I have made you and I will carry you; I will sustain you and I will rescue you."

(Isaiah 46:4)

I love the poem "Footprints", also known as "Footprints in the Sand." Who doesn't? I mean, we can all relate to times in our lives when we can clearly see the footprints of God walking beside us, and other instances when there is only one set of prints in the sand. These are the moments when it's easy to think we're walking alone. But do you know what? Our Heavenly Father is carrying us, as a loving parent does.

Recently, my niece shared with me a different perspective to footprints in the sand. Her husband had finally returned home after lockdown regulations in South Africa during the COVID-19 pandemic had eased slightly, permitting business travel. As they walked along the beach in front of their seaside home one afternoon, she noticed their footprints from the previous day's walk. His prints were big and deep; hers small and shallow. She couldn't help thinking how her husband's tracks in the sand were so like his life—everywhere he walked, he left a profound and lasting impact.

This, in turn, shifted her thoughts to the insignificance of her own life—or so she thought—her prints small, shallow. What mark could she possibly be making in comparison to those large, sunken imprints?

As she shared the feelings of her shortcomings with her husband, he reminded her that for his single stride, she'd taken three steps. She couldn't possibly take gigantic or deep steps because she was so busy meeting everyone's needs that she had to tread swiftly and lightly. Her impact was just as profound as his, only in a different way.

As she pondered this, considering her husband, the Lord reminded her that those deep footprints were also made by one bearing a heavier load.

Later they came across a third set of prints, ones even smaller than her own. Shallower imprints in the sand. A child's—one who had tried walking in *her* footsteps, and couldn't. To that child, *her* prints were as big, and probably as deep, as her husband's were to her.

Each one of us has an individual path to tread, one that God has laid out for us since before the foundation of the world. Some of us will leave a deeper impression than others, but some of our life journeys will touch more lives. We should therefore never compare our footprints to those of others—we're all different, with different purposes.

Have you ever thought about what kind of footprints you're leaving behind as you walk through life?

 "Lord God, help me to tread only in the footprints of Jesus. May the marks I leave behind as I traverse this life be worthy of the One whose steps I am following. Amen."

7

Reflections in the Fog

"So we fix our eyes not on what is seen, but on what is unseen, since what is seen is temporary, but what is unseen is eternal."

(2 Corinthians 4:18)

Growing up, the best part of our annual holiday at the sea for me and my siblings was watching anxiously for that first glimpse of the ocean.

"Ten points for the person who sees the sea first," we'd squeal in delight, in those exact words, as my dad's Land Rover made its way over the green hills of Natal toward the coast. This was about the time we all sat up and took notice because there was one particular spot on the outskirts of Durban where the road came over a rise and a smidgen of the vast blue ocean was visible. Still is today, over five decades later. And that was the moment we had all waited twelve long hours for.

While visiting the West Coast recently, I often stood on the back stoep* of my niece's house, gazing at the ocean and the horizon. Some days the straight blue line between the water and the wild blue yonder was clearly visible. Sometimes ships altered the horizon's shape while other days dolphins frolicking in the bay drew my attention away from the skyline. Toward evening, the setting sun colored both water and sky with pink, purple, and orange hues. And in the dark of night, boat lights twinkled far out at sea, reminding me that the expanse of water was still there.

But there were days when thick fog clouded the view, blotting out everything in sight. Only my imagination and memory were left to picture what lay beyond the misty curtain of gray.

Isn't this so like our walk with God? There are times when we can see Him as clearly as that horizon on a cloudless blue day. Other times He chooses to reveal Himself in glorious splendor, as beautiful and magnificent as the sunsets He drapes over the earth at the end of each day.

In those days when you can see nothing at all and it seems as if He's no longer there, remind yourself that God has promised He will never leave us, never forsake us. Is your path unseen and you can't see through the fog of your circumstances? Hold on tightly to the nail-scarred hands guiding you back toward the light. When we face our darkest nights, He shines bright through the blackness to let us know He's still there.

* *Stoep*: South African veranda

"Abba, it's so easy for me to forget the things You have done for me, so easy not to remember Your life-giving promises. Remind me when there seems to be no hope, when I'm tempted to give up or give in, that You are with me. All. The. Time. Thank You for Your loving assurances. Thank You that Your love is everlasting. Never let me forget that, Lord. Remind me often—please—because I am weak, and I am only human. Amen."

Thank You for Reading!

I hope you enjoyed reading *Reflections from the Ocean (and Surrounds)*. If you did, please consider leaving a short review on Amazon, Goodreads, or Bookbub. Positive reviews and word-of-mouth recommendations count as they honor an author and help other readers to find quality Christian books to read.

Thank you so much!

If you'd like to receive information on new releases, cover reveals, and writing news, please sign up for my newsletter on my website.

About Marion Ueckermann

A Novel place to Fall in Love

USA Today bestselling author MARION UECKERMANN's passion for writing was sparked when she moved to Ireland with her family. Her love of travel has influenced her contemporary inspirational romances set in novel places. Marion and her husband again live in South Africa and are setting their sights on retirement when they can join their family in the beautiful Cape.

Please visit Marion's website for more of her books:
www.marionueckermann.net

Contact Marion: marion.ueckermann@gmail.com
You can also find Marion on social media:

Other Books by Marion Ueckermann

FICTION

CONTEMPORARY CHRISTIAN ROMANCE

CHAPEL COVE ROMANCES
Remember Me *(Book 1)*
Choose Me *(Book 4)*
Accept Me *(Book 8)*
Ride with Me *(Book 10)*
Releasing 2020
Trust Me *(Book 13) Releasing 2021*

Other books in this tri-author series are by
Alexa Verde and Autumn Macarthur

MOSAIC COLLECTION
Before Summer's End
(My story in this anthology is *In an English Vintage Garden*)

THE POTTER'S HOUSE
SHAPED BY LOVE
Restoring Faith *(Book 1)*
Recovering Hope *(Book 2)*
Reclaiming Charity *(Book 3)*

A TUSCAN LEGACY
That's Amore *(Book 1)*
Ti Amo *(Book 4)*
Other books in this multi-author series are by:
Elizabeth Maddrey, Alexa Verde, Clare Revell, Heather Gray, Narelle Atkins,
and Autumn Macarthur

UNDER THE SUN
SEASONS OF CHANGE
A Time to Laugh *(Book 1)*
A Time to Love *(Book 2)*
A Time to Push Daisies *(Book 3)*

HEART OF ENGLAND
SEVEN SUITORS FOR SEVEN SISTERS
A Match for Magnolia *(Book 1)*
A Romance for Rose *(Book 2)*
A Hero for Heather *(Book 3)*
A Husband for Holly *(Book 4)*
A Courtship for Clover *(Book 5)*
A Proposal for Poppy *(Book 6)*
Releasing 2021
A Love for Lily *(Book 7)*
Releasing 2022

HEART OF AFRICA
Orphaned Hearts
The Other You

HEART OF AUSTRALIA
Melbourne Memories

HEART OF IRELAND
Spring's Promise

HEART OF CHRISTMAS
Poles Apart
Ginger & Brad's House

PASSPORT TO ROMANCE
Helsinki Sunrise
Soloppgang i Helsinki

(Norwegian translation of Helsinki Sunrise)
Oslo Overtures
Glasgow Grace

ACFW WRITERS ON THE STORM
SHORT STORY CONTEST WINNERS ANTHOLOGY
Dancing Up A Storm ~ *Dancing In The Rain*

BOX SETS

The Way to the Heart
(The Other You, Ginger & Brad's House, Melbourne Memories, A Courtship
for Clover)

Jayne
(A Match for Magnolia, A Courtship for Clover, That's Amore)

Michael
(Restoring Faith, Reclaiming Charity, Ti Amo)

Those Blue Tuscan Skies
(A Romance for Rose, That's Amore, Ti Amo)

The Potter's House
[Books 7, 14, and 21]
(Restoring Faith, Recovering Hope, Reclaiming Charity)

Seasons of Change
[Books 1-3]
(A Time to Laugh, A Time to Love, A Time to Push Daisies)

Love is all around
[A collection of Christmas stories from around the world]
(A Husband for Holly, A Time to Love, Ginger & Brad's House, Melbourne
Memories, Poles Apart)

399

Seven Suitors for Seven Sisters
[Books 1-4]
(A Match for Magnolia, A Romance for Rose, A Hero for Heather, A Husband for Holly)

NON-FICTION

Bush Tails
(Humorous & True Short Story Trophies of my Bushveld Escapades *as told by Percival Robert Morrison*)

POETRY

Glimpses Through Poetry
[Bumper paperback of the four e-book poetry collections below]

GLIMPSES THROUGH POETRY
My Father's Hand

My Savior's Touch
My Colorful Life

WORDS RIPE FOR THE PICKING
Fruit of the Rhyme

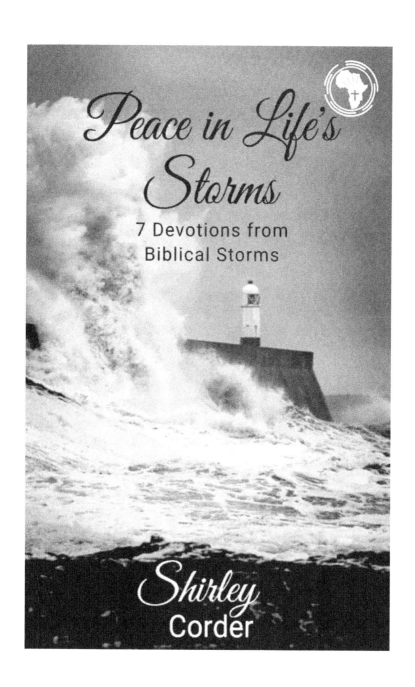

Peace in Life's Storms

7 Devotions from Biblical Storms

Shirley Corder

PEACE IN LIFE'S STORMS

Cover Art © Shirley Corder
Cover Image Lighthouse © Marcus Woodbridge @ Unsplash
Praying Hands: coolvectorstock @ 123rf
Africa Icon: Shirley Corder

Edited by Paula Bothwell @ PBProofreads

These devotions are written in American English. Where African terms are use they are clarified.

Newsletter

Would you like to be among the first to know when a new book is coming out?

Sign up for my newsletter and you will receive:

»A free book

»Snippets of personal news

»Updates on my latest writing project

»Sneak Peeks into my books

»Recommended reading material

»Occasional free offers or competitions

Emails normally only come to you every two weeks or longer. I will not fill your inbox with SPAM, nor will I pass on your address to anyone else. You may also unsubscribe at any time. Sign up on my website.

Visit me at my **website**, https://www.shirleycorder.com.
Email: WriteToInspire@shirleycorder.com

Acknowledgments

Grateful thanks as always to **my husband, Rob,** for all his encouragement and for freeing up so much time for me to write.

Huge thanks to **Dianne Marie Andre** for her critiques, edits, and friendship, from across the world.

Thank you to those who beta-read or edited this book: **Shirley Crowder, Judith Robl, Arlene Johnson, Dianne Marie Andre, Pam Corder, Larissa Clark, Rob Corder**.

Thank you to **Paula Bothwell** @ PBProofreads for doing the final edit.

Thank you to all **the photographers** who make the result of their talents available to the public on the Internet.

Thank you to **the members of my Book Brigade** who encourage me and help me to get the word out about my books.

Mostly, all thanks and praise to my **Heavenly Father** who is always there to breathe peace into the storms of my life.

To all those who are on the frontline of the battle against the COVID-19 storm that has gripped the world in its global pandemic.

Thank you for all you have done, and continue to do.

The Lord bless and strengthen you, and grant you His peace.

Table of Contents

Introduction

In turbulent times, there's always a place of peace, a starting point of healing through Christ.

In April 2020, our minister of health in South Africa announced on national television "the COVID storm is upon us." Even now, across the globe, this deadly virus seems to be intent on destroying our planet. This storm may not have been caused by out-of-control weather, but it is wreaking havoc on a far wider scale than most physical storms.

In Scripture we read of a number of storms that made such an impact we still remember them thousands of years later. Where it is normal to have calm *after* a storm, like when Jonah took a dive, we may also experience peace *during* the storm, like Job. There are also times when we experience calm *before* the storm, like when Jesus lay sleeping in the stern of a boat.

Whatever type of storm you face right now, God wants to grant you His peace. Come along with me as, over the next seven days, we learn more from seven storms recorded in God's Word.

The Biggest Storm of All Time

"He will cover you with his wings; you will be safe in his care; his faithfulness will protect and defend you. You need not fear any dangers at night or sudden attacks during the day or the plagues that strike in the dark or the evils that kill in daylight. A thousand may fall dead beside you, ten thousand all around you, but you will not be harmed. Whoever goes to the LORD for safety, whoever remains under the protection of the Almighty."

(Psalms 91:4-7 GNB)

"Make sure properties are secure and all loose materials around dwellings are tied down or brought inside before the approaching storm." I had just read these words as South Africa was being warned of a "monster" cold front and storm advancing on our land.

I watched online as a massive truck and trailer were blown over by the wind on a stretch of road well known to me outside of Cape Town. This extreme weather was scheduled to reach where I live in Port Elizabeth in about two days. Already, the normally blue sky was white with heavy cloud cover, and the wind here in the "Windy City" of South Africa was starting to roar. By the next day, it would probably not be safe to go for walk to the beach for fear of being blown over. This seemed to be yet another reason why we need to stay home! As if COVID-19 were not enough.

In Genesis chapters 6-9 we read of another world-changing event, one so massive that it destroyed almost all mankind. Nothing microscopic here! We're talking about the biggest flood on record.

Can you imagine the terror among the people of Noah's time as they began to realize that the gigantic monstrosity their strange neighbor had been building for years was actually going to be needed? Noah's weather forecast had given them plenty warning, but still they probably laughed and jeered. It is likely that they humiliated him and his family and carried on with their partying and lawlessness.

And then the rains came. And the storm began.

Did the skies turn black? Rumble with a thunder never heard before?

What was the crowd's reaction when rows of animals lined up in neat groups, without any type of herding, in order to enter the ark?

At what point did panic set in? When did they start to believe?

Sadly, it was too late. All but Noah's family perished in the worst human calamity ever.

I wonder if Noah ever asked himself what would happen if the storm never arrived? God had said to him, "*I am going to bring floodwaters on the earth to destroy all life under the heavens, every creature that has the breath of life in it. Everything on earth will perish*" (Genesis 6:17 NIV)

But what if God had changed His mind? After all, He is God. What if there were no floodwaters? Yet, Noah clearly sensed God's peace throughout his building operations. He believed God would be with him, no matter what the future held.

As I look at the havoc and devastation caused by out-of-control wind or other weather patterns . . . or invisible-to-the-naked-eye viruses, I cannot help but wonder. We are so dependent upon God's laws of nature. We rely on going to bed one night and waking the next morning to a world that's operating the same way as it was the night before. Yet, at the present time, we may go to our beds one evening and awaken to a whole new reality as COVID-19 continues to cause disease that thrashes the continents, and governments take drastic steps to try and flatten the curve of the pandemic. No sooner are lockdown regulations eased than they seem to be reinstated. Governments face an ongoing juggle between the economy and people's lives.

Here in South Africa, we have been in lockdown since March 26, 2020, and at the time of this writing, there is no end in sight. We are cresting the second wave, and already the doom-sayers are predicting a third.

How are you spending your days? Do you ever wonder if something you have spent hours on may turn out to be a waste of time? That's where it's helpful to pray that God will grant you His peace, not only in the build up, but also when the storm eventually arrives, as He did for Noah

That ark must have been the most horrific lockdown of all time. The family spent a year in a smelly ark full of animals. At least I get to spend lockdown in my own home with doors and windows I can open.

When God finally gave Noah and his family seven days notice, saying, *"Go into the ark, you and your whole family"* (Genesis 7:1), I'm sure Noah breathed a huge sigh of relief. And yet, what of all the crowds of onlookers? What would become of them? Many of them would have been friends or even relations.

It was too late. Noah had doubtless tried his best to convince them of their need to repent, but now it was between them and their Creator. God had spoken, and Noah and his family had to obey. They had to step through the only door into the ark. There was no back entrance.

The only assurance we have of salvation is if we enter the door God has provided for us—the door of Jesus Christ. Only through Him, do we receive a guarantee of eternal life. Unfortunately, some of God's own people have tested positive with COVID-19. Some have passed into His presence. But at least, if they have entered into the salvation offered by Jesus, their death will be a move into eternal life in Heaven.

Are you safely on the ark of salvation? Are you certain?

There must have been times when Noah and his family wondered if it was really worth it. Would it ever end? But God saw them through. The eight people who entered the ark before the arrival of the biggest storm of all time, stepped outside a year later to see God's glorious rainbow. A sign of God's peace.

We too, can experience His peace through storms and other times of trauma, if we only go through the door, and put our trust in Him.

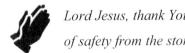 *Lord Jesus, thank You for Your goodness in providing me with a place of safety from the storms of life, and a door that will lead me to Heaven. Lord, please help me to take that step through the door. Encourage me to stretch out a hand to those around me that they may come too. Please grant me Your peace before and during any storms You plan to take me through.*

Lord, I plead for an end to this pandemic. But please help me to learn lessons from this time, and help the people of this world to listen before it's too late.

In Jesus' Name,

Amen.

-2-

Blessed Be Your Name

"When the storm has swept by, the wicked are gone, but the righteous stand firm forever."
(Proverbs 10:25)

On Friday, March 6, 2020, my husband and I went to house-and-doggy sit at a friend's home. She directs a local senior choir of nearly forty people and I am her deputy. At the point she left on vacation, we had heard of a deadly and novel coronavirus and the havoc that it was causing in many parts of the world, but it was nowhere near South Africa. So it wasn't an issue for us.

The very night our friends left, my husband and I heard on the news that the first case of COVID-19, the disease caused by the dreaded virus, had been identified in our country. The man had just returned from Italy. At least he was on the other side of South Africa from us.

That week, I conducted a concert with the choir at a home for the handicapped. The following week, we were due to hold a concert in a large retirement village. The audience plus choir would comprise around a hundred folk over the age of seventy. After watching the news over the next couple of days, we decided it wasn't safe to go ahead with the concert, so I canceled. That was early in April 2020. The choir hasn't met since, and at the time of writing this, there is no indication when we will be able to.

The COVID-19 storm had indeed come upon us. No warning—and with devastating consequences.

In what scholars believe to be the oldest book of the Bible, we meet Job, a wealthy man of integrity and father of ten. In a matter of a few hours, he lost all his donkeys, oxen, and field hands, in a horrific farm attack. Then a tremendous storm erupted. Lightning killed his sheep and shepherds. As if that wasn't bad enough, a marauding army made off with his camels and massacred their keepers.

While Job was still trying to wrap his head around all this, he heard that a tornado had struck the house where his seven sons and three daughters were partying. It killed them all. No warning—with devastating consequences.

My mind is blown away when I read how he got to his feet, ripped his robe, shaved his head, and fell to the ground and *worshiped*. In other words, he observed all the customs of those days to grieve—and then he worshiped. Wow! *"The LORD gave and the LORD has taken away; may the name of the LORD be praised"* were his now-famous words (Job 1:21).

When COVID-19 first hit our country with a strict lockdown, a common reaction was "This is going to be tough—but I can do it!" Social media was full of the activities people got involved in. They spring cleaned their homes, scrubbed their cupboards, and sanitized their shelves. Craft cupboards were repacked (speaking personally) and new systems devised for storage. People exchanged recipes and took to the kitchen. Here in South Africa, many of the stores opened for on-line purchases, and I moved into the world of cybershopping.

But as time went by—and we've been in lockdown since March 26, 2020—the cleaning and tidying frenzy grew old. One day, I had a minor meltdown and felt discouraged. What was wrong with my faith? Then I discovered this was the norm. People started off well, but the stress factor and staying home started to cause breakdowns in control.

The same seemed to happen to Job. The poor man developed a dreadful skin disease that nearly drove him crazy. His wife kept criticizing him. His three closest friends came to support him. Initially they sat in supportive silence. Then, oh my goodness . . . Talk about, "With friends like these, who needs enemies?" (You can read their words in the book of Job.)

The amazing faith of Job resonates as you see his peace through his entire trauma. Despite all the dreadful suffering, he never doubted God's authority in his life.

Eventually, Job lost his composure, and who could blame him? *"I can't stand my life—I hate it[2]!"* (Job 10:1 MSG). Have you ever felt that way? Can you identify with him? Have you coped well with a storm in your life, perhaps COVID-19 or perhaps a different one, only to melt down at some point? Probably more than once? The good news is that's normal. God understands. Job told God just how he was feeling, and that's something we need to do. "Lord, I feel . . ." Be honest. After all, He already knows.

We are a social people. The lockdown and social distancing protocols being demanded of us by governments across the world are hard. Think how much more difficult they would be if we did not have God to talk to.

Despite all his heartache and hardship, Job had close communication with God. For us too, this can be a time when we experience God's presence in a special way. Is there something you can do to draw closer to God at this time, in the midst of your storm? Is there a way you can handle your emotions better, and perhaps prevent another meltdown?

Despite everything, Job defended God against his friends. Note that he never doubted God was in control. In fact, he *blamed* God for much of his hardship. He stopped trying to be stoic and spread his entire situation before God.

Perhaps now is the time you need to stop trying to keep that brave face in place, and admit to the Lord that you badly need Him to shelter you from the storm raging round you.

In the middle of yet another violent storm, God intervened. He somehow brought healing and the man of God was able to rise up from the ashes and move on with life. He once again became a very rich man, and lived long enough to see four generations of family. And the book of Job ends with the words, "Then he died—an old man, a full life" (Job 42:17 MSG).

There is a well-known phrase, often wrongly attributed to the Bible: "This too shall pass." It was true for Job. And it's true for us today.

COVID-19 will eventually pass. So will whatever other storms you face right now. But it will be easier to cope with while it continues to rage, when we rest in the arms of an almighty God. No matter the severity, we can receive His peace in the storm.

 Lord, thank You for the reminder that life isn't always fair. There are dynamics to this story, and in my life, that I don't understand. But You created me, and You have a plan for me. One of these days, I will see that this storm has passed over and my life is again at peace. Until then, may Your Name be forever blessed! And help me to walk through the storm experiencing Your perfect peace.

In Jesus' Name,

Amen.

-3-

The Sound of Silence

[Nothing] "will be able to separate us from the love of God that is in Christ Jesus our Lord."
(Romans 8:39)

I have a nephew in the theater business. Just prior to our national lockdown, he and his group of musicians produced a CD based on Simon and Garfunkel songs. Of them all, my favorite is "The Sound of Silence." Yet, until recently, I didn't stop to analyze the title. The *sound* of silence? How can you *hear* silence?

A man in the Old Testament did. His name was Elijah.

The story began with a showdown on Mount Carmel between God's prophet Elijah and the prophets of Baal. The nation of Israel was no longer worshiping only Yahweh, but several other gods, especially Baal, the fertility god.

Elijah and King Ahab gathered the people on the mountain to settle an age-old question. "Who is God?" Baal? Or Yahweh?

Today, people face the same question. Who is God? Is it Buddha? Or

Mohammed? Is he in the jihad, in sports heroes, or even in the mirror?

"How long are you going to sit on the fence?" Elijah demanded. *"If GOD is the real God, follow him; if it's Baal, follow him. Make up your minds!"* (1 Kings 18:21 MSG).

Nobody said a word. Not a sound. Silence.

Can you *hear* that silence?

Some probably wished someone would speak up for God . . . as long as it wasn't them. Others wanted to praise Baal, but they didn't dare. Silence. A silence impregnated with guilt and fear.

Who is God? I wonder what answers we would get if we walked around the streets today and asked folks randomly? "Who is God?" How do *you* answer?

I so often hear people complaining that God doesn't answer their prayers, and I want to ask them, "Have you really listened? Have you listened *through* the silence? Do you have the faith to believe He will answer?" Maybe they would believe if He answered them immediately. That would be nice. Answers to prayer may involve a wait. But He will answer. Why am I so certain? Because He is God. And He promises in His word that He will hear and answer the prayers of His people.

Yesterday, a man who claims to be a Christian said to me, "I don't always believe God's Word. I'm sorry, but there are parts of the Bible I don't accept."

I replied, "There are parts of the Bible I don't understand—but then I'm not God. And aren't you glad about that?"

How about you? I'm sure there are parts of the Bible you don't understand. Me too. But do you believe it is God's Word? In which case, how can it contain falsehood? My small grandchildren wouldn't understand any book I wrote. I don't write for children. But that doesn't make the words untrue.

We don't have to understand. We just need to listen. Even when it's silent.

Elijah knew God would keep His word, and he had obviously heard from God. Otherwise, I'm sure he wouldn't have taken the crazy actions he did.

First, he laid down a challenge. Whichever god could start fire would be the true God. The people agreed, and each group prepared a huge mound of firewood and slaughtered an ox.

The Baal prophets went first. They prayed. They cut themselves with swords and knives. They used every trick they knew, but nothing happened.

Eventually, it was Elijah's turn. He first built an altar of twelve stones. He surrounded it with a trench and laid the firewood on top. He added the dissected ox to the pile. Then he commanded people to fill the trench with water and drench the meat and firewood. (Nothing like making it tough for God!) See what I mean? He was pretty sure God wanted him to do this—and he knew that God would answer his prayers.

He stood back and prayed, asking God to send fire. *Immediately* fire fell from Heaven and burned up the entire sacrifice, including the water in the trench. The people fell on their faces and acknowledged, "The Lord! He is the true God!"

After dealing with the wicked prophets of Baal, Elijah turned to Ahab. *"Rain is on the way,"* he said. *"I hear it coming"* (1Kings 18: 41 MSG). The prophesied storm arrived fast. The sky grew black. Clouds blew furiously across the sky. A cloudburst of rain cascaded from the heavens. I imagine for them it was rather like the arrival of the COVID-19 storm was to us. In December 2019, we were confronted with a breakout in China. Within a matter of months, the entire world was under a cloudburst of virus. People were dying in the thousands.

You would think after this amazing series of miracles, Elijah would have been on cloud nine. But as is so often the case after a wonderful mountain-top experience, Elijah seemed to have lost his way in the melee. When Jezebel, Ahab's wife, heard what had happened, she set out to avenge the death of her prophets. And the great man of God fled! He went into isolation, hiding in silence under a juniper tree, virtually suicidal.

Days later, God sent an angel to supply his needs, and told him to make his way to Mt. Horeb, a forty-day journey away. Upon arrival at Mt. Horeb, Elijah had a night's sleep before the Lord ordered him to stand on the mountainside outside the cave where he'd spent the night. Suddenly, Elijah had to grab for support as a tremendous wind tore across the face of the mountain, shattering rocks. Next, the mountain shook violently with a strong earthquake. Elijah dove back into the cave to shelter from the horrendous storm. *What was God doing?* The mountainside broke out in flames. Would the fire consume him like it had the ox just over a month before?

Then he heard something. So soft it was like a whisper on the breeze.

He covered his face with his cloak for protection against flying debris and stepped to the entrance of the cave. He listened intently. And he heard the sound of silence. A silence followed by the voice of God. *"What are you doing here, Elijah?"* (1Kings 19:13).

I often wonder how I would have answered that question. Elijah poured out his sad story to the Lord. And the Lord answered.

The COVID-19 storm is wreaking havoc across the globe. It's frightening. For the first time for most of us, we are being called to stay in isolation. Home alone. Unable to spend time with loved ones. Maybe this is a good time to ask you how you're spending your time? Are you setting aside more time to read God's word?

We are so privileged in our society to have the Internet. Several times a week, my husband and I go onto the Web and listen to sermons or studies by fabulous people of God. There's far more time for that today.

And sometimes, isolation and quiet is when we can best hear God speak. Not in the crowds. Not over the news. Certainly not on social media. But in the sound of silence.

Lord, thank You that You are the One True God, and that I can believe Your Word—even the passages I don't understand. Thank You that whether I am in isolation, or even quarantine, You are not. Thank You that I can hear You—even in the sound of silence. Nothing can separate me from You.

In Jesus' Name,

Amen.

-4-

Running from God

"But with shouts of praise, I will offer a sacrifice to you, my LORD. I will keep my promise, because you are the one with power to save."
(Jonah 2:9 CEV)

The greatest "storm" I ever faced occurred in 1997/98 when I battled with aggressive breast cancer with glandular involvement. Several times it looked as if I was losing the fight. On many occasions, people wondered aloud why God had sent such a dreadful disease my way or why He had allowed the devil to put it upon me.

To me, the question wasn't about why, so much as how this fitted in with God's plan. Whether God had given it to me (and I preferred to think He hadn't) or whether He had allowed it, what was the purpose? I believed God had a plan for my life (Jeremiah 29:11), so how did this cancer fit in? Was it my time to go home to the Lord? Then why this way? Was there a lesson to learn that would change my way of life? Until I knew the outcome, I resolved to fight this storm in every way I could.

In the Old Testament, we read of an interesting man who initially didn't attempt to fight a storm even when it threatened to take not only his own life, but many others' too.

Jonah was a man of God on board a ship bound for Spain. Nothing wrong with that, except that God had explicitly told him to go to the city of Nineveh, in the opposite direction.

Why would Jonah do such a stupid thing? Well, he later admitted he didn't trust God. God wanted Jonah to warn the people of Nineveh that He'd had enough of their wickedness and He was going to take action. Jonah felt afraid God wouldn't follow through and would show the Ninevites mercy. Then what would happen to Jonah? So he played the "What if?" game—and decided to run away. He paid probably a considerable amount of money and climbed on board the ship and off they sailed. *Did he really think he could hide from God?* He must have been desperate because the Jewish people of his time generally viewed the open sea with dread, seeing it as a place of terror and chaos.

God had no intention of letting Jonah escape. The trip started out to be fairly uneventful but then we read *the LORD hurled a great wind upon the sea, and there was a mighty tempest on the sea, so that the ship threatened to break up* (Jonah 1:4 ESV). Strong language! The word "hurled" is one used for a warrior throwing a spear. God was not going to be mocked by Jonah!

The storm was of such magnitude that the experienced mariners panicked. They did everything in their power to save the ship, *hurling* their cargo overboard to lighten the load. They also prayed—each to their own god. So often, a tremendous crisis causes people to turn to religion. Even today as COVID-19 rages across the globe, more and more people are crying out to their gods for help. And they're rowing as hard as they can, tossing out things they now realize are not helping them.

And all this time, while the mariners were trying to save the ship, where was Jonah? Did he come to help? Nope. As a paying passenger, he was taking it easy—sound asleep on his bunk. Perhaps his rebellion against God had worn him out. Whatever, the captain had to go and wake him, and order him to get up and pray! So often at a time of life-threatening crisis, the ungodly will see the need for spiritual intervention. How sad that the suggestion didn't come from the one who worshiped the *true* God!

In their desperation, the sailors resorted to a common practice and cast lots to find out who was to blame—and the lots fell on Jonah. As they cross-questioned him, Jonah gave them a lesson in theology. They didn't want theology! They wanted help. At last, Jonah took responsibility for his actions and offered himself as a sacrifice. "Throw me into the sea," he said.

What storm are you facing right now? How do you know what to do next? Do you feel like asking someone to throw you into the sea? That sounds pretty desperate to me. Are you doing all you can to get free of the storm, relying on your own efforts? Are you following government protocols? Or following doctor's orders? Or are you listening to people and their conspiracy theories—no matter what sort of storm you're dealing with? There's always someone who will spout nonsensical theories and suggestions, all designed to appeal to the easy way out. What *should* you be doing?

The men didn't want to throw Jonah into the raging waters, and they tried all they could to gain control of the ship. Then, using stilted words, they called on God—the Lord Himself—and prayed for forgiveness before throwing Jonah into the turbulent waves.

Immediately the storm ceased. *Wow!* Just like that. Those hardened mariners were over-awed by the One True God. They worshiped Him and made promises to Him.

I wonder if they spotted the gigantic sea creature that suddenly surfaced long enough to swallow the man they had just thrown overboard. God had already organized an unusual mode of transport to get His disobedient prophet to the required destination. How amazing that the One who had sent the storm had known ahead that Jonah would need rescuing at that precise spot on the ocean, at that exact moment in time.

There are people out there who share the same storm as you. They need to know about your God. Are you sleeping through the storm? Or are you talking theology? Neither will help. What can you do that will introduce people to the One True God?

What is even more amazing is that, despite his outright disobedience, God still used him to bring about a mighty revival in the city of Nineveh. But that's another story which you can read in the rest of the book of Jonah.

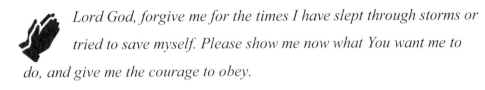 *Lord God, forgive me for the times I have slept through storms or tried to save myself. Please show me now what You want me to do, and give me the courage to obey.*

In Jesus' Name,

Amen

-5-

Asleep in the Stern

"Then he got into the boat and his disciples followed him. Suddenly a furious storm came up on the lake, so that the waves swept over the boat. But Jesus was sleeping. The disciples went and woke him, saying, 'Lord, save us! We're going to drown!' He replied, 'You of little faith, why are you so afraid?' Then he got up and rebuked the winds and the waves, and it was completely calm. The men were amazed and asked, 'What kind of man is this? Even the winds and the waves obey him!'"

(Matthew 8:23-27)

The Lord was exhausted. So were the disciples, and more than a little overwhelmed by all they had witnessed that crazy day. Jesus had healed a soldier's servant without even going near his home. He'd raised Peter's mother-in-law from her sickbed so completely she was able to get up and make them a meal. He'd driven out evil spirits and healed many other people from different diseases. He'd preached to a multitude and then given private lessons to his disciples. Now He needed a break.

"Let us go over to the other side," He suggested, stepping into the boat bobbing on the Sea of Galilee. The disciples followed. Note that crossing the lake was Jesus' idea. Unknown to the disciples, He was needed on the other side. Meanwhile, He needed rest.

After resting his head on a pillow in the stern, in seconds He was fast asleep.

Then the storm hit. Sudden storms were common on that lake, but this was a real humdinger. The waves broke over the fishing boat. Even those disciples who were seasoned sailors could not control the boat. Should they wake Jesus? He was so tired. The storm would surely wake him. They continued to struggle without success.

Surely the Creator of the world knew a storm was coming?

Yes, He probably *did*, but it caused Him no concern. Why would it? God wanted Him to cross the lake. Why would a storm change that plan?

Could He not have delayed His departure? The answer is a simple, "No." If they'd stayed where they were, the crowds would not have left Him alone. He also had a divine appointment on the other side of the lake.

My husband and I always pray before setting out on a trip, but Jesus didn't hold a prayer meeting before they set off. He settled down in the stern of the boat for a snooze. The nap became a deep sleep. So deep, He wasn't even aware of the gigantic storm, or that the boat was in danger of sinking.

Eventually, the experienced sailors knew they had to wake Him or they would all drown. One has to wonder why they thought He would be able to help. They were the fishermen, not Him.

When they managed to rouse Him from His deep slumber, His first reaction seems to have been annoyance. "Why are you so afraid?" He demanded. Rubbing the sleep from His eyes, He stood up, rebuked the winds and waves, maybe for disturbing His rest or for scaring his friends? And the storm immediately died down.

Wow! I'm not surprised the disciples were amazed. I would have been too. But the question that bothers me is why Jesus was annoyed when they woke Him.

I doubt He was upset they asked for help. They were in deep trouble. He would have expected them to call. So why His reaction? Take a closer look at their words. "We're going to drown!"

They had Jesus on board! He wanted to go to the other side of the lake. *Why would they drown?*

Do we sometimes look around at the fearsome floods, the earthquake shaking our land, the novel coronavirus sweeping the world, then rush to the Lord? That's great. That's what we're supposed to do. But are we saying, "Help! We're all going to die!"? Are we forgetting Who is in the boat with us?

Are we praying, "Lord, don't You care that this microscopic virus is threatening the entire human race? Don't you see that our kids are being sent back to school when it's not safe? Are you aware we might run out of toilet paper? Don't you care?"

I don't believe Jesus is asleep right now. But when He one day steps forward to stamp out this beastly virus, or whatever storm is threatening you right now, is He going to ask you where you put your faith? In the government? In the health leaders? In the television news? In your friends?

Or in Him?

Sometimes faith is not performing great acts, like building a boat or evangelizing a city. Sometimes it is having the ability to bask in God's peace even amid a storm.

COVID-19, or whatever other storm you are dealing with, may still escalate before being brought under control. But our Savior will never lose control. As long as you stay in the boat, you can experience His peace.

How do we remain in the boat? By not giving up. By spending time getting to know the One who is there with us.

Dear friend, set aside time to read some good Christian books, talk to Him in prayer, and spend time in worship with hymns and songs from the Internet or your music player. And above all, don't keep trying on your own. Call out to Jesus for help.

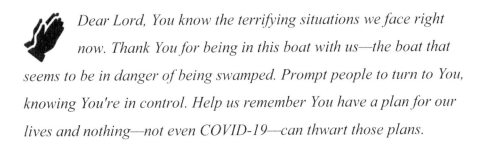 *Dear Lord, You know the terrifying situations we face right now. Thank You for being in this boat with us—the boat that seems to be in danger of being swamped. Prompt people to turn to You, knowing You're in control. Help us remember You have a plan for our lives and nothing—not even COVID-19—can thwart those plans.*

We ask this In Jesus' Name,

Amen.

-6-

Walk on Water

"Come," [Jesus] said. Then Peter got down out of the boat, walked on the water and came toward Jesus. But when he saw the wind, he was afraid and, beginning to sink, cried out, "Lord, save me!"
(Matthew 14:29-30)

I've never tried to walk on water—but I know what it's like to get out of the boat in scary circumstances.

My husband, three kids, and I were spending a few days in a cottage at a resort on the side of a large dam in what was then called Rhodesia. The other side of the lake was dense bush believed to be inhabited by terrorists.

One afternoon, we decided to treat the children and signed up for a cruise on a locally owned ferry. We had a wonderful time. Far away, on the shore of the resort, people *braaied* (barbecued) while others enjoyed a game of cricket or sunbathed.

We were enjoying ourselves on the water when suddenly, the engine cut out. The captain and his assistant worked feverishly, trying to get it started once more. They had no anchor.

"The ferry's drifting," someone said in alarm. Sure enough, the ship was bobbing gently on the surface of the water, drawing closer to the far side of the lake. The area that was suspected of harboring terrorists.

The captain stood and grabbed his radio. Minutes later, men at the distant resort started running for the water. An armada of small motor-boats sped toward our stricken vessel.

As they pulled up alongside, the men on board started to lower the women and children onto the rocking little ships. Fear gripped my throat. I didn't want to leave the apparent safety of the ferry without my husband and take off with strangers on a little ship. But I was given no option, and minutes later my children and I were bouncing over the now-choppy water on the way to safety. After some time, we all made it safely to shore, including the menfolk. We clustered together, watching as a bigger motorboat towed the ferry back to land. The boys enjoyed their adventure. My daughter and I? Not so much.

Two thousand years ago, Jesus had the most awful day. It started with the news that King Herod had beheaded his cousin, John. Jesus withdrew by boat to an isolated place with only His disciples. He needed some alone time. But the crowds followed him. Instead of sending them packing, Jesus showed them compassion and healed their sick. Then He taught them. At suppertime, He got the disciples to sit them down, and He fed the entire multitude of well over five thousand people using just five loaves of bread and two fish—the miracle we know of as "The Feeding of the Five Thousand."

Come night time, Jesus must have been exhausted—and He still hadn't had His alone time. He sent the disciples off on their boat to the other side of the lake. He headed up the mountainside to finally spend private time with His Father.

During the night, He was aware that the disciples were struggling with a severe storm that had arisen. So, near dawn, He set out to help them— walking on the water. *How crazy was that?*

The disciples spotted this ghostly figure coming towards them through the mist and the rain, and they were terrified.

I don't blame them! I was scared when I saw all the small boats coming to our rescue. I don't want to think how I would have reacted if one of our rescuers came *walking* to our stranded ferry!

Jesus called out to reassure them. Then Peter—bold, impulsive Peter who acted first and thought later—shouted back, "If it's You, call me to come to You." Notice that Jesus was too far away for the disciples to be certain of His identity.

As soon as the Lord called him, Peter swung his leg over the side of the boat and took a step on the water. Then another step. He was walking on water! He had almost reached Jesus when, as Peter often did, he made a mistake. He looked down at his feet.

At that moment, two things happened.

First, he had to take His eyes off Jesus to look down.

Second, he saw the size of the waves. *Oh, yikes!* What was he doing, walking on this turbulent water? He couldn't walk on water!

Jesus didn't actually ask Peter to do any great work of faith. He only told him to "come." Peter only needed to step out of the boat and walk.

No big deal. He walked all the time. The miracle was the surface he walked on. And that was God's responsibility.

We know the story. Peter started to sink, and Jesus stretched out his hand to fish him out of the water and deposit him back in the boat. So Peter had walked a fair distance on the sea before his mind pointed out he couldn't do it! When he stepped out of the boat, he was far enough away that he couldn't recognize Jesus. Yet here he was close enough for Jesus to fish him out the water. *How long does it take to sink?* Think about that. Peter was right up next to Him.

Note that Peter only stepped out when Jesus called him to do so. Have you ever been told to "step out in faith" when you have had no clear direction from God? *Don't do it!* Don't step blindly out of the boat, unless God gives the command. Not your neighbor. Not some politician. *God!*

When you become aware of the size of the waves—the spread of COVID-19, the fury of the storm raging in your life—what does that mean? Have you perhaps taken your eyes off Jesus? Or are you being so bombarded by news, you cannot help but see the size of the waves? Here in South Africa, we are experiencing the "second wave" of COVID. The *world* is even calling it a wave! How can we best keep our eyes on Jesus and get them off the waves?

 Lord Jesus, thank You that when You call us to step out in faith, we can do so with the assurance that You will not let us sink. Lord, please help us to differentiate between Your voice and the many

other voices that urge us to take steps "in faith." Grant us Your peace,
even during the midst of the storm.

In Jesus' Name,

Amen

-7-

When There's No Hope

"[God said] 'Don't be afraid, I've redeemed you. I've called your name. You're mine. When you're in over your head, I'll be there with you. When you're in rough waters, you will not go down. When you're between a rock and a hard place, it won't be a dead end."
(Isaiah 43:1-2 MSG)

Have you ever been seasick? I have, and it's a horrible feeling. I'm sure Paul and his friends, Aristarchus and Luke, were seasick on their voyage to Rome. Even the hardened sailors on board were probably sick This was among the worst of all storms. Not only were they seasick, they doubted they were going to make it to land.

Julius, the centurion of the elite guard who was in charge of the three friends as well as other prisoners, seems to have been a nice guy. He showed kindness to Paul. However, when Paul had advised him to halt the journey in a safe harbor because of dangerous weather ahead, the centurion disregarded the advice, and all 276 travelers set to sea.

A gentle, southerly wind soon turned into a north-easterly hurricane. It went on for days. Things got worse on board, and the ship took a violent battering. The sailors threw the cargo and ship's tackle overboar

Eventually, everyone, including Paul and friends, gave up all hope of survival (Acts 27:20).

When people face life-threatening situations in their lives, like COVID-19, they often want to give up. *What's the point in fighting this? We have no hope.*

Storms and trials can make us bitter—or better. In which camp are you right now?

Paul kept remembering God's promise that he would go to Rome. God makes promises, but He has His own timing. Two years earlier, the Lord Himself stood near Paul and told him he was going to testify in Rome (Acts 23:11). It had taken two years, but finally it was God's timing, and Paul was on his way. He pointed out to the men that his faith was in the Lord, and that he believed God would keep His Word.

If you have given your life to the Lord Jesus, you too have the assurance that He has a plan for your life. God purchased you with the blood of His own Son. You are of great value to Him. He will not let you perish.

One night, in the midst of the storm, an angel appeared to Paul and said, "Do not be afraid, Paul. You must stand trial before Caesar; and God has graciously given you the lives of all who sail with you" (Acts 27:24). It's interesting to notice the angel's opening words: "Do not be afraid!" Paul was human, and he was afraid. He hung onto his faith, but that didn't stop him from being scared.

During life-threatening storms in our lives, it is okay to be afraid. But we must hang onto God's promises, and trust Him to carry us through.

Can you think of any ways can you "toughen up" to deal with whatever storm you're going through at the moment?

Paul assured the crowd that they would all be saved, but he urged them to look out for land where they could run the ship aground.

After enduring this dreadful storm for two weeks, they spotted land. Once again, Paul encouraged them. The sailors had not been eating, possibly due to feeling sick, or perhaps because of their fear. Paul urged them to eat as they would need their strength. He broke bread in front of them and gave thanks to God, and they followed his example.

Our neighbors need us to set an example. So do our families, and our work colleagues. How will they know how to trust the Lord during a crisis if they don't see our example? And how will you be able to give them that example if you don't go through the storm yourself? Paul had warned them not to sail, so he could have taken the attitude of, "On your own head be it! I told you it wasn't safe. Now see for yourself." But he showed his love and concern for these men who needed the Lord and encouraged them to put their trust in Him. Notice he didn't try to preach to them. He didn't deliver a condemning speech. He was practical. "You guys need to eat!"

Who do you know who needs encouragement? How can you best help them to experience God's peace? Sometimes the best thing we can do for someone in a crisis is to be practical. What do they need? How can you help them cope? The opportunities to share your faith may come later.

Oh, that we might remember Paul's example. For sure, many of those we are in contact with do not deserve God's forgiveness . . . but then, neither do we. We need to pray for those who have ignored us or even hated us. Let's show them God's love by example.

Afraid the prisoners might escape, these rough men of the seas showed their true colors. They decided to kill all the prisoners, including Paul who had saved them. But Julius came to the rescue. He ordered all those who could swim to jump overboard and make for the shore. He told the others to get on planks or pieces broken from the ship and use them as life rafts. All 276 made it to safety.

Sometimes our lives seem to be surrounded by broken pieces. We can't see the way through the storm or crisis. We long for the security that's found in larger objects—like the ship. But the ship broke. Our faith is not in the big things. It is in God Himself, and He may well use little things to bring about our safety.

 Lord, as we journey through storms in life, help us to keep our faith in You. Remind us of Your promises. Encourage us, Lord, please, and help us to show Your love and peace to those around us.

In Jesus' Name,

Amen.

Do You Know God?

If you are out when a thunderstorm hits, your first reaction is to dive for shelter, to find a safe place. Do you have a safe place to hide from whatever storm life may throw at you? Do you have a secure assurance that the Lord of all creation is there, ready and willing to provide you with that safe place?

When the storm strikes, be it nature on the rampage, a global pandemic, a life-threatening disease, or any other type of human disaster, it is too late to go looking for shelter. You need to be certain now that you have a place with God, that He is waiting with arms open wide to shelter and reassure you.

One day you will meet Him face to face, perhaps as a result of a storm, or maybe because your time on earth has come to an end. One thing is sure. That moment will arrive. Are you certain you will be accepted into His Kingdom?

Sometimes the weather gurus get it right when they predict storms. Sometimes they don't. At the beginning of 2020, no one predicted the immense COVID-19 storm that was about to sweep the world.

Don't wait for another cataclysmic event to descend on your life. If you're not already 100% sure of your relationship with the Lord, please don't put it off one more moment.

I encourage you to use the format of A, B, C, D, and make sure you have a safe place to shelter from whatever storm that may come your way.

Accept that you are a sinner. Scripture tells us we are *all* sinners. Romans 3:23 tells us "all have sinned and fall short of the glory of God."

Believe Jesus Christ is the Savior who loved you so much that He gave His life for you. Jesus said, "I am the way and the truth and the life. No one comes to the Father except through me" (John 14:6).

Confess to Him that you have not been fully surrendered to Him and ask for His forgiveness. "If we confess our sins, he is faithful and just and will forgive us our sins and purify us from all unrighteousness" (1 John 1:9).

Dedicate yourself to the Father as your God, Christ as your Savior, and the Holy Spirit as the Wind beneath your spiritual wings. Jesus said, "whoever hears my word and believes him who sent me has eternal life and will not be judged but has crossed over from death to life" (John 5:24).

You can use your own words, or you can use these:

 *Father God,*

I have done things which have separated me from You. Please forgive me.

Lord Jesus, I believe You are the only way to God.

I give myself to You now, and I ask You to help me follow You for the rest of my life.

Holy Spirit, please lift and support me as I seek to walk closer to God.

From this moment on, I will seek to walk with You and bring glory to Your name.

I ask this in Jesus' name and through the power of the Holy Spirit.

Amen.

If you've prayed this prayer for the first time, I would love you to make contact with me. You can **email me** at writetoinspire@shirleycorder.com or contact me through my **website**, https:///shirleycorder.com.

If you have enjoyed this book, I'd really appreciate you leaving a short review on Amazon.
Thank you!

Keep in touch and hear when I have other books coming out. All you need do is sign up for my newsletter on my website.

About the Author

Shirley Corder is a retired nursing sister (RN), pastor's wife, and cancer survivor (1997). She is an internationally well-known devotional writer.

She is the author of a number of books, some of which are available in print as well as electronic format. She has also contributed to thirteen anthologies and other books not to mention many devotional and inspirational articles through the years.

Do visit her on her website, shirleycorder.com, or drop her an email a writetoinspire@shirleycorder.com. She'd love to hear from you.

Shirley and her husband, Rob, enjoy life in the beautiful seaside city of Port Elizabeth, South Africa. They have three married children and ar grandparents to six special young people across a wide range of 21 years

Website: https://shirleycorder.com
Email: shirley@shirleycorder.com

More Books by Shirley

7-DAY SERIES

God in the Unexpected: In these seven devotional readings, Shirley Corder encourages you to look for God in the Unexpected.

A Mother's Heart: Being a mother isn't for sissies. But in these seven short stories, Shirley Corder shares some life-lessons drawn from her own life that will draw you closer to God, and to your children.

The Boat that Saved the World: God tells Noah He is going to put an end to the human race. It gets worse. He wants Noah to build a boat to start over. How crazy is that? Read the story from Noah's perspective.

7 Animals of Africa: In these seven devotions, Shirley Corder shows you God's hand at work in the lives of seven amazing animals. You will receive encouragement to draw close to the God of creation. Available as part of this boxed set.

90 DAY BOOKS

God in Africa - 90 Days in the Land of Majesty and Mystery*: Available as an Ebook or paperback at this link, or the paperback direct from the author. If you want to know the real Africa beyond the extreme images, violence, and hunger narratives often portrayed in the media, then this book is for you.

Strength Renewed - Meditations for Your Journey through Breast Cancer: An encouraging 90-day devotional book for those facing cancer. The book is published by Revell Publishers and is available in e-format or paperback.

OUT OF THE SHADOW SERIES

The *Out of the Shadow* stories are creative non-fiction and include inspirational reflections. They are ideal for devotional times with the Lord, or for use in Bible Study groups.

EVE ~ Mother of All: Join Shirley as she draws Eve out of the shadow of the garden and shows her as a real flesh-and-blood woman. If you've ever felt overwhelmed by your situation, or faced impossible challenges, this book is for you.

MIRIAM part 1 ~ Devoted Sister: The little girl who watched her three-month-old brother sail in a basket boat on the crocodile-infested River Nile lived her life under the shadow of her younger brother, Moses. If you have a gifted sibling or friend, or if you battle with feelings of inferiority, you will enjoy this book.

MIRIAM part 2 ~ Gifted Leader: As Miriam comes out of the shadow of her two brothers, Shirley shows us how she becomes a gifted leader in her own right. If you have struggled with criticism over a woman's role in the Church, this book is for you.

NAOMI ~ Beloved Mother-in-law: Join Shirley as she eases Naomi out from the shadow of her daughter-in-law, Ruth. If you've faced tragedy or felt afraid for the future, this is the book for you.

Thank You for Reading
IN ALL THINGS
13 weeks of devotions from Africa

by

Christian authors of Africa

SHIRLEY CORDER

ASHLEY WINTER

ANNA JENSEN

YVONNE TIPPINS

CRYSTAL WARREN

DERYN VAN DER LANG

DIANNE J. WILSON

VAL WALDECK

VIDA LI SIK

ANN GOODFELLOW

MARION UECKERMANN

If you've received a blessing through these readings, we would very much appreciate you leaving a review on Goodreads, Amazon, or on any other social media.

Printed in Great Britain
by Amazon

63328980R00254